Am I Codependent? And What Do I Do About It?

Answers and Solutions for Codependent Relationships with and Without Substance Abuse

AM I CODEPENDENT? And What Do I Do About it?

Kara Lawrence

Published by Diana King, 2019.

While every precaution has been taken in the preparation of this book, the publisher assumes no responsibility for errors or omissions, or for damages resulting from the use of the information contained herein.

AM I CODEPENDENT? AND WHAT DO I DO ABOUT IT?

First edition. September 14, 2019.

Copyright © 2019 Kara Lawrence.

Written by Kara Lawrence.

© **Copyright 2019 - All rights reserved.**

The content contained within this book may not be reproduced, duplicated or transmitted without direct written permission from the author or the publisher.

Under no circumstances will any blame or legal responsibility be held against the publisher, or author, for any damages, reparation, or monetary loss due to the information contained within this book, either directly or indirectly.

<u>Legal Notice:</u>

This book is copyright protected. It is only for personal use. You cannot amend, distribute, sell, use, quote or paraphrase any part, or the content within this book, without the consent of the author or publisher.

<u>Disclaimer Notice:</u>

Please note the information contained within this document is for educational and entertainment purposes only. All effort has been executed to present accurate, up to date, reliable, complete information. No warranties of any kind are declared or implied. Readers acknowledge that the author is not engaging in the rendering of legal, financial, medical or professional advice. The content within this book has been derived from various sources. Please consult a licensed professional before attempting any techniques outlined in this book.

By reading this document, the reader agrees that under no circumstances is the author responsible for any losses, direct or indirect, that are incurred as a result of the use of information contained within this document, including, but not limited to, errors, omissions, or inaccuracies.

Table of Contents

Introduction

Chapter 1: Distinguishing Codependency from Dependent Personality Disorder

Chapter 2: Defining Codependency: The Origins and Evolutions of the Term

    Addicted to Your Partner
    Other Relationships

Chapter 3: 10 Critical Warning Signs of Codependency

Chapter 4: Codependency with and Without Substance Abuse

    Gambling
    Sex
    Food
    Shopping
    Work

Chapter 5: Childhood: Developmental Conditions Contributing to Codependency

Chapter 6: The One Root Cause of Codependency

    Where Does the Pain Come From?
    How Good Turns Bad
    Through the Eyes of Codependency
    Future Impacts

Chapter 7: Why Codependency Can Easily Lead to Abuse

- Control
- Narcissism
- Past Abuse

Chapter 8: Psychology of Being Controlling: When the Abused Becomes Abusive

- Sides of Abuse
- Empath/Narcissist Abuse
- Manipulation Tactics
- Detachment

Chapter 9: Empath and Narcissistic Relationships

- How Labels Are Hindering
- Where Codependency Fits In
- Label Culture

Chapter 10: Solutions to Codependency Issues: Must I End My Relationships?

- Relationship Reform

Chapter 11: Exercises

- Positive Affirmations
- Inner Child Work
- Detachment
- Boundaries for Shame
- Positive Surroundings
- Self-Expression
- Loving Yourself

Chapter 12: Happy Being Me

Self-Soothing
Enjoy Alone Time
Separation from the Outcome

Chapter 13: Life After Codependency

Getting Help

Conclusion

Signs to Pay Attention To
Dangers Involved

References

Introduction

Adopting codependent behavior within your relationship can start as a simple attraction to your partner. You might love a person so much that you only want to spend time with this person. This is natural during the honeymoon stage, but when the codependency begins to impact other areas of your life, you might encounter problems. Those who are severely codependent might be unable to shop for groceries on their own. Even the simple task of getting ready in the morning might revolve around what the other person is doing. Codependency often stems from a sense of insecurity. Perhaps you felt unsure of yourself prior to the relationship, and now that you are experiencing this kind of happiness, you might feel that you can only reach this point with codependency.

The concept of codependency also revolves around boundaries. If you are unable to set boundaries, you will fall into behaviors that are solely molded after what your significant other prefers. Even if they do not directly ask you to act a certain way, you might subconsciously be acting on things that will clearly only benefit them. A lack of boundaries can also lead to your partner using you. Giving up on this choice puts you in a position where you have no more decision-making options. This behavior can also manifest itself in the opposite way—you might feel so codependent that you will seek control over what your partner is doing. No matter how it presents itself, codependency can become unhealthy very quickly.

It is a category that you might feel you do not belong in, but you would be surprised how common it is for people to end up in codependent relationships. Because a relationship revolves so much around having a close bond with your partner, it can become easy to form these codependent habits. If you often find yourself in relationships that end up in dysfunction, but you do not know why, you should observe the stance that you take. Do you make decisions for yourself, or do you prefer to go along with what your partner suggests? Alternatively, do you try to take control over a situation before your partner has the chance to think for himself? Both of these examples can indicate that you are a codependent person.

Being able to clearly identify any signs that you are codependent is going to help you. Once you can spot the problem, you will be one step closer to reaching a solution. Codependent relationships can be rebalanced, but it takes awareness and effort on both ends. By working together with your partner, you will be able to single out certain behaviors that indicate that things might be biased. You can break down the root cause of each one in order to determine why it happens. From there, solutions can be presented. As long as you are able to work with your partner through every step of the way, a healthy relationship is possible.

Many people recognize that they are in a codependent relationship, but they go about fixing it the wrong way. Those who simply try to change their partner in order to fit the narrative end up staying in unhealthy relationships. Your relationship can be different; by using methods that are proven to improve the quality of relationships, you can fix the issue so that it will not return in the future. Changing select behaviors is only a temporary fix. Plus, it becomes unfair if only one person must change. A balanced relationship revolves around compromise.

AM I CODEPENDENT? AND WHAT DO I DO ABOUT IT?

The amount that you give should be the amount that you receive in return.

Your childhood can shape the way that you function in a relationship. Depending on what you have experienced as you grew up, these traits can remain as you enter adulthood. A person's past can tell you a lot about their habits in the present. If a child was abandoned or left alone a lot, it makes sense that they would turn into a codependent adult. While this is only one example, there are others that can lead to codependency. The behaviors that we display are often acted upon in a cycle. If we tend to gravitate toward people who use us, you can expect the same results when you begin dating. By becoming aware of your codependency, you are giving yourself a chance to break this cycle and to strive for a healthier relationship.

Studies have shown that those who make it a point to work on themselves before entering long term relationships end up staying happier in those relationships. If you are facing insecurities, this can become distracting (even detrimental) in your current relationship. You must be able to be accepting of the person that you are before you can learn to accept someone else, flaws included. A lot of us fear to be alone, but what we don't realize is that we can actually grow and make our future relationships even better when we take the time to get to know ourselves. Once you make it a habit to take care of yourself and to understand yourself, you will find yourself applying the behaviors toward your partner.

Despite the current situation that you find yourself in, this guide is meant to help you get to the next step toward a healthy relationship. By using the tools that are provided, you will feel as if you have control over your own life and your own decisions. By taking a step back and looking at codependency from another perspective, you might realize what it is that you need to change in order to reach your ultimate happiness. Those with this knowledge are able to think critically and act accordingly. Not only will these tools help you in your current relationship, but they will also help you in making important decisions that have the ability to shape the rest of your life.

Those who choose to ignore codependency tend to become stuck in the behavior for a long time. The longer that you are involved in a relationship that lacks balance, the harder it can feel to end it or fix the problem. If you are tired of experiencing failed relationships or temporary connections, making a change is going to be exactly what you need. Some people who remain stuck in codependency can also experience worse problems, such as substance abuse or even becoming a victim of abuse. There are so many reasons why it is a smart decision to rebalance your level of codependency, but the ultimate reason is definitely to improve the quality of your life. No one deserves to be stuck in a rut of misery, feeling as if there is no way out. There is always a way to make a change.

Stop waiting around for the "right time" to make a change because the very best time is right now. By reading this guide, you are already on your way to your first step toward overcoming codependency and gaining knowledge about the subject. After you finish this book, you should feel confidence behind each decision that you make. You will find the joy in your relationship; some of you will even rekindle the joy that was originally felt from the beginning of the relationship. It is possible to gain freedom from codependency, no matter what situation you are currently in!

Chapter 1: Distinguishing Codependency from Dependent Personality Disorder

When you are in a relationship, there is going to be a natural lean toward codependency. Your partner is someone that you should trust and enjoy being around, so it makes sense that you would want to spend lots of time with that person. Sharing decision-making responsibility is one of the best parts about being in a relationship, especially for those who tend to struggle with them. Having someone with you can be nice when you are navigating through your daily life, and there is nothing wrong with this. The behavior becomes codependent when it prohibits you from making your own choices. Whether you are placing this restriction on yourself to please your partner, or you are being controlled, the behavior becomes a problem that can be hard to reverse.

Dependent personality disorder, or DPD, is a serious mental illness. One of the main symptoms of DPD is the inability to be alone. Although it takes a professional to diagnose this disorder, it is still important that you are aware of it. DPD will cause a person to measure their happiness based on another person. If their partner is unhappy, then the individual feels like they also need to be unhappy. Even when behaviors are hurtful, a person suffering from DPD will not be able to just walk away from the relationship. There is no sense of desire to express any personal needs or wants, and because of this, anxiety can arise.

Some other symptoms of DPD are having trouble with decision-making, passiveness in all situations, not wanting to remain alone for long periods of time, and not taking personal responsibility for decisions. A lot of this probably sounds like codependency to you. While the two are similar, there are a few details that distinguish them. DPD occurs when a person is relying on the care that the other person provides them. In codependency, a person will act this way because of a mutual sense of needing one another. Even if neither of these cases is true within a relationship, both can become detrimental to the person experiencing the skewed perception.

There are certain instances where DPD will actually prevent someone from leaving their house, even if they truly want to, simply because their significant other is also home. An extreme sense of needing to be cared for is present in a relationship like this. Being able to pinpoint certain childhood experiences that have led up to this point is definitely going to be useful when treating DPD. Because it is such an intense illness, it is also often deeply rooted in the past. The behaviors go beyond

AM I CODEPENDENT? AND WHAT DO I DO ABOUT IT?

wanting to be with your partner all the time and instead shift focus on *needing* to be with that person in order to function on an everyday basis. If a person with DPD is not able to accomplish this, then they might begin to unravel.

Codependency is not actually an officially diagnosable condition. It is not formally recognized in the DSM-V manual that psychologists use when making a diagnosis. The phrase is actually rather informal, and it was originally used when describing a person's abusive relationship with alcohol. Though the terms dependent personality disorder and codependency are often used interchangeably, this is not correct. Know the difference between the two before you decide which one you identify with. With the former, only a licensed professional is going to be able to correctly diagnose you. Remember that a mutual dependency is what truly separates the disorder from the behavior.

In codependent relationships, normally one person will rely on the other emotionally, while the other person acts as an enabler. Codependent relationships are definitely not one-sided, and both parties have to be willing to accept that the behavior is damaging before they can make any changes that will last. In order to further understand the differences between DPD and codependency, it is important that you also take a look at the differences between being dependent and codependent:

Dependent: In a dependent relationship, there is mutual being placed on the relationship. While happiness can exist within the relationship, it can also be found in other activities and people. For example, hanging out with a friend should be able to bring someone happiness just as their significant other can. The levels of communication in the relationship are balanced and open. If there is a problem, both people should be able to express their concerns and be able to work through issues together. The sense of reliance on one another appears to be mutual, and both people feel happy with the dynamic.

Codependent: This relationship looks different. There is a level of care involved, but that care is one-sided. Normally, only one person places a large amount of value on how happy their partner is. It is also common for this person to be the only one who chooses to do things that will result in their partner being happy. There is a sense of disregard for oneself, choosing the happiness of another over the way that they are personally feeling inside. There might be sacrifices made at the expense of the codependent individual. This person is also unlikely to place time in any other outside interests or relationships. All of these time and energy goes straight into their partner, often diminishing who they are as a person.

It is clear to see that being in a dependent relationship is the healthy version of codependency. Knowing that you place this mutual trust in one another can be a great feeling. Think about the dynamic of the relationship that you are in. It should be clear to see if the feeling is mutual or not. If you ever feel that you are making more sacrifices than you should, it is important that you speak up about the issue. You should feel comfortable coming to your partner with anything that you would like to discuss. In a healthy relationship, these problems are worked through together in order to come up with a solution that will benefit both of you while fixing the issue.

This book is going to cover multiple topics, two of them being emotional dependency and addiction recovery. Emo-

AM I CODEPENDENT? AND WHAT DO I DO ABOUT IT?

tional dependency is the behavioral trait that is found in codependent relationships as well as those suffering from DPD. It has the ability to transform someone into a completely different person that only chooses to focus on the happiness of the person that they are dating. Remember, it is not something that you must place blame on yourself if you find that you are either codependent or suffering from DPD. Both of these conditions are able to escalate rapidly. What was once a healthy and balanced relationship can shift into something that is toxic simply because one person isn't able to cope on their own.

Placing blame on yourself, or even someone else is not going to fix the problem. This is only going to create tension. A trick to solving problems within your relationship is going to be found in being patient. You must remember that overcoming codependency takes patience for yourself and for the other person involved. If you only skim over the steps, you are not going to create a solution that lasts. You need to aim for serious fixes, not temporary ones. A lot of people find themselves stuck because they can only accomplish the latter. You will find strength in reading this guide, and it is likely that you will learn things about yourself that you never knew before. Know that it is okay to be in a committed relationship with someone while also still being your own person with your own interests.

It is possible to become addicted to being codependent. This is yet another way that the behavior can become detrimental. By definition, addiction is the physical and psychological inability to stop doing something. In turn, this can become damaging for everyone involved. Being addicted to codependency is a tense way to live. The person is always going to feel as if they are on edge, waiting to decide what they would like to do based on the actions of another person. If their partner decides to stay at home, they will stay at home. If their partner decides to watch tv, they will watch tv. It is a desperate need to be on the same page as your significant other, but so much that it actually creates a sense of falseness.

For the same reason that any addict cannot just simply stop, a codependent individual isn't going to stop at another's request. Being addicted to codependency gives the person a purpose, and they are going to feel as though they cannot walk away from this purpose. For those who are especially insecure, being codependent can actually provide somewhat of a confidence boost. We all know that it feels great to feel needed in life, and this is the exact feeling that a codependent individual can become addicted to. Even relationships that start out healthy have the potential to end up this way. Behaviors that aren't changed can evolve into codependent ones, which will then evolve into an addict. This is a dangerous pattern to allow. If you find that you are in a situation like this, it isn't too late to get help.

As we will discuss later on in this book, getting help is one of the hardest yet best things that you can do. To be able to stop and admit that you need help is an act of true courage. Addictions aren't easy to overcome, especially when you live with them. Unlike substance abuse, what you are addicted to is readily available around you all the time. The feeling wears off faster because it is something that you constantly have access to. When you are codependent and dating someone, you become infatuated with them. In your eyes, they can do no wrong. This is why it does not feel like an addiction. To you, this is just your normal level of care.

AM I CODEPENDENT? AND WHAT DO I DO ABOUT IT?

Another way that addiction can present itself is in the form of alcohol abuse. This type of addiction can occur when the individual isn't getting what they desire out of the relationship. Maybe they act codependent but come to realize that their partner does not need them as much as they do. This can create an instant wave of insecurity to wash over a person who is involved in codependency. By clinging onto a crutch, the person who is acting codependent will feel as though they have something that they can always rely on. By choosing to drink, they are choosing to take control over some aspect of their life. While this doesn't make sense to a lot of people, to the addict, this is the only way to feel as though they have any type of control in their own life.

This is another topic that this book is going to explore in greater detail. Being able to recognize the signs of alcohol is just as important as being able to recognize the signs of codependency. A lot of the time, the two can go hand-in-hand. Ultimately, they both involve regaining control and having a purpose in life. While they have unfortunate consequences, a person with an addictive personality isn't going to be able to see the dangers in this behavior. To them, this is a decision that is necessary for survival. They aren't going to want to listen to logic when they are already deep in either addiction. If you or someone you know is currently experiencing this, getting help is always going to be the best way to overcome it. Only a professional will be able to correctly diagnose addiction and come up with a treatment plan.

Chapter 2: Defining Codependency: The Origins and Evolutions of the Term

In order to fully understand codependency, it is a good idea to learn about its origins. The Alcoholics Anonymous program was first created in 1936. It is a 12-step program that is still being used to this day for treating addiction. The program focused on the 12 steps that would assist an addict with overcoming addiction, focusing on the actual addiction itself. Before the creation of AA, it was thought that those who were addicted to alcohol simply had a lack of self-control. People saw it as a weakness when someone simply couldn't stop drinking. AA changed the way that we view addiction. It taught people that addiction is very real and very consuming.

By the '70s, various alcohol treatment providers began to criticize the outdated methods of AA. They believed that the program was too one-dimensional to maintain lasting results. It was after this that AA transformed into a program that treated more than just the disease. Family relationships and social dynamics were then taken into consideration to better understand the illness. Professionals saw that there was a large instance of those who were inclined to stay with chemically dependent partners despite the hardship. Programs were also created for these individuals to help assist with their own personal struggles, as well as the struggles of being with an addict. It was after this that the programs were able to see a greater success rate with fewer instances of relapse.

Treatment programs began using the term "chemical dependency" to describe both alcohol and drug addictions in 1980. Because they often had more similarities than differences, the programs believed that this was a better way to describe both. Drug programs were being refined to utilize the same 12 steps that AA used, but this time, it was for the purpose of treating drug addictions. All of this treatment fell under the same "chemical dependency" category. To say that someone was "co-chemically dependent" became difficult to express. This was the way that professionals used to define those who were dependent on a person who was chemically dependent. So for that reason, the term was shortened to "codependency." It is a term that we are all familiar with today.

In 1984, S. Wegscheider-Cruise, founding chairperson of the National Association for Children of Alcoholics, claimed that a person can be codependent if they: are in love or in a relationship with an alcoholic, had a parent or parents involved in alcoholism, or were raised in a way where emotions were repressed. It was around this time that treatment centers realized that they had to provide programs for people who fit these criteria, too. By modern-day definition, the term codependent can both refer to the person who is addicted as well as the person who is involved with someone who is addicted. Today, we tend to use it interchangeably to describe both.

Addicted to Your Partner

IT IS POSSIBLE TO FORM an addiction to another person. Those who are in this predicament might feel like they are unable to function without their partner. The codependency becomes their only way of life. Through trying to please this person or control a relationship, the codependent individual gains a sense of self-worth. Even if, deep down, they do have desires of their own, they will never act on them. Think of this as a sacrifice that the person was never asked to make. These behaviors have the ability to strip a person of their own identity. This is how it can become so easy for the codependency to spiral out of control. A simple tendency can evolve into a full-blown problem.

Remember, the word codependent signifies that both parties play a role. It is a mutual decision to stay in the relationship, despite any underlying feelings or thoughts. The person who is destructive will continue with their ways despite any hurt that they cause toward their partner. Both people need one another in order to continue the codependent relationship. It is going to be a relationship that is filled with dysfunction to other people who are onlookers, but to those in the relationship, they will not see that anything is wrong.

Both parties become so comfortable with the uncomfortable that they won't have any desires to change anything about the dynamic. The dysfunctional individual is usually going to be the more dominant one. This is the person who is going to act exactly how he or she wants to act without considering the consequences of their actions. The codependent individual is going to support his or her partner no matter what, even when their behavior is questionable or embarrassing. There is an undying need to be there for their partner and actually be with them.

This is the most modern evolution of the term codependency. When you use this term, the example that was given is normally the one that people think about. To onlookers, it can often look as though the codependent individual is trapped or scared to leave the relationship. Inside though, they might not even have any desire to leave their partner. It is a complicated situation to understand when you are not in it. This is why it is important to be patient if you do know someone who is codependent. It is not as simple as getting up and walking away, just as it is not as simple for an alcoholic to stop drinking.

Other Relationships

CODEPENDENCY DOES NOT discriminate. It can happen to anyone, young or old. Depending on your past experiences, your fear of abandonment will vary. Those who have been abandoned at a young age are naturally going to have a fear of this as they grow up. The way that this is dealt with ultimately decides if it is going to become detrimental to the person or not. With proper counseling, a person can grow to learn how to live without fear of abandonment. If they do not get help though, it can transform into an inability to maintain a healthy relationship. Those who are codependent have usually experienced patterns of codependency throughout their lifetime.

A parent/child relationship can become codependent. In the exact same way that a codependent relationship is formed, parents and children can create a bond that is toxic. This is something that might start early on and then never fully go away as the child grows older. As stated, the more something is practiced, the harder it becomes to stop the habit. This type of relationship is damaging because it can cause developmental delays when a child is codependent toward a parent. The child might grow to become an adult who is incapable of making decisions and might even refuse to leave home in fear of leaving their parents.

In some cases, codependency can happen within a friendship or even a mentor type of relationship. When someone does something to help you, this is a point where it is easy to become attached to that person. Those who experience close friendships might thrive off of this feeling and will never want to lose it. A codependent friendship might look like one where the pair is always together, but one person is using the other person to his or her advantage. Remember, there is normally a codependent individual and a dysfunctional individual that feeds off of having someone in their life who will never leave.

Chapter 3: 10 Critical Warning Signs of Codependency

With codependency, there are signs everywhere. You might not be able to see them if you are in a relationship like this yourself, but they can be very apparent to other people. Consider the following warning signs when trying to determine if your relationship is indeed a codependent one:

- **You Are Dating an Addict**: Being with an addict comes with a large sense of responsibility attached. Even though it is up to the individual to make their own choices in life, it also says a lot about you if you choose to be with a person like this. Not everybody who is dating an addict is automatically codependent, but the relationships tend to shift in this direction before too long. Because your partner has a focus on something that is so destructive, you become an enabler to them. With your support, even if you are not directly supporting the addiction, you are giving them the security that they need in order to never change their ways. With a codependent relationship, the person with the addiction does not fear loss. Instead, they will likely feel power in knowing that they have you.

- **You Help More Than Necessary**: Do you find yourself going out of your way, even if it is majorly inconvenient for you, to help your partner? This can be something as simple as driving to the other side of town to go to the store for them, even when they work right across the street. Actions like this are unnecessary, and they can indicate that codependency is occurring. Listen to what the people around you are saying. If you have done something similar to this, it is likely that those closest to you are going to take notice. Has anyone mentioned to you that you do a lot more for your partner than you should? Take these words into consideration.

- **You Often Feel Anger or Resentment**: Despite all that you choose to do for your partner, you will feel a sense of anger that strikes you from time to time. You might even bring up how much you do for this person in order to make them feel bad for you, even when you weren't asked to do these things in the first place. Codependency places a sense of

AM I CODEPENDENT? AND WHAT DO I DO ABOUT IT?

urgency behind your actions that no one is really enforcing except yourself. You might feel like it is your duty to have everything that he or she wants and needs, but then you end up feeling resentful toward them afterward. This feeling can become overwhelming to the codependent individual, often causing an internal struggle that is left to be dealt with alone.

- **You Feel Responsible for Your Partner's Actions**: Basing your reasoning on the fact that you love this person, you might feel like their actions are your responsibility to take on. An example of this would be when your partner gets into an argument with his or her friend. You might feel the need to step in and smooth things over for your partner because you feel that it is your place to do so. To you, everything that your partner does has a direct impact on you in some way. You might feel the need to change things about your own life in order to become more accommodating to how your partner acts.

- **You Frequently Worry About Your Partner's Issues**: Whenever your significant other experiences a problem, you might tend to make it your own problem. While the intent behind this action is helpful, it can quickly become detrimental to you. Being able to let go while your partner sorts through his or her own issues is an essential part of not being in a codependent relationship. You should be available for support, but not to take on the entire burden of their situation. This becomes unhealthy, and with codependency, he or she will keep placing this burden on you when they realize that you are willing to take it.

- **You Allow Hurtful Behavior to Occur**: Being put down doesn't seem like a big deal to you anymore because it probably occurs a lot if you are in a codependent relationship. You don't feel bothered by insults or passive-aggressive behavior because you secretly feel as though you deserve this treatment. Someone who is trying to cope in a relationship like this will often let poor behavior continue simply because he or she does not want to upset their partner in any way. They would rather allow themselves to be treated worse if it means that their partner would feel better.

- **You Are Affected by Your Partner's Mood**: You might be in a fantastic mood from the great day that you've just had but you've come to find out that your partner had a bad day at work. This can all change once you find this out. It is natural to feel empathetic toward your significant other. This is a healthy display of affection, but when it has the ability to completely derail you from your own emotions, then it becomes a problem. You should be able to support your partner while still maintaining an independent stance. Just because he or she is in a bad mood does not mean that you need to be in one too. You might feel like it only makes sense to suffer because they are suffering, too. This is how codependency can trick us into changing when we really don't want to.

Some people actually may be hyper sensitive to the moods of others and can even experience absorbing stress and negative emotions when they don't want to. I have written a separate companion book entirely on this subject titled, "Empath Awakening," by myself, Kara Lawrence. In it, you can find the tools to stop absorbing the hurtful emotions of others if you believe yourself highly sensitive or empathic.

- **You Always Vocalize What You Are Doing**: Your actions revolve around the fear of being accused of wrongdoing. Even when it isn't necessary, you will probably find yourself narrating your actions to your partner in order to seek his or her approval. Many who are in codependent relationships feel like it is their partner's right to have control over every situation. By telling your partner what you are doing, even when they do not ask, this is your way of submitting to their needs. If something you do becomes inconvenient for them, you will be a lot more likely to stop because you are already seeking their approval.

- **You Don't Often Get Your Needs Met**: Meeting your partner's needs is a priority but having your own met is merely an option. This is the core of a codependent relationship. You might lead yourself to believe that it is okay that your needs aren't being met, but you might secretly wish that your partner were more attentive. Because there is no balance within a codependent relationship, this happens pretty frequently. One person is always going to be wishing that they had more of their needs met, but likely won't do anything to change this.

- **You Diminish Your Own Feelings**: Even if something your partner does really upsets you, usually you are the first to play it off. Dismissing your feelings comes naturally because this is what your partner normally does to you. Nothing that you are experiencing could possibly be a big deal, at least that is what your codependent mindset tells you. For this reason, a lot of individuals who are in this situation tend to suppress a lot of negativity inside. This remains within like a ticking time bomb, just waiting for something to set it off.

While the examples listed above are not all of the warning signs to look out for, they make up a core group of behaviors that you will likely find within a codependent relationship. If you feel like you can relate to this list, an evaluation of the current relationship that you are in could be necessary. When you evaluate something, no action is required to be taken. Try not to put pressure on yourself by making it a point to make a drastic change within the relationship. An evaluation is nothing

AM I CODEPENDENT? AND WHAT DO I DO ABOUT IT?

more than a critical observation. While you focus on the dynamic between you and your partner, really try to break down each behavior.

Pay attention to anything that elicits a response within you, this includes both negative and positive actions. A lot can be said about the things that make you upset and the things that make you happy. Even if you do not act on these feelings, try to think about what caused them. It can be hard to pinpoint a reason at first because you are likely used to grouping your feelings with your significant other's. Think of your evaluation as a diary entry that only you get to write in. It can be very difficult for someone in a codependent setting to think independently, but it is necessary. Do your best to sort through your feelings.

You are likely going to place blame on yourself for every negative reaction that you feel inside. Try to break through this way of thinking. Believing that everything is always your fault places a huge burden on yourself as you are trying to navigate through your own life. It is an unnecessary hardship that you are placing on yourself, all for the possibility that it might make your partner happy in some way. Remember, your happiness matters too. You are just as worthy of feeling positive emotions as your partner is. In order to change the cycle, a sense of self-love must be felt. It's easy to be hard on yourself, but how does it feel to love yourself?

Once you have done your observations, take a look at any patterns that might be present. Are your feelings triggered by anything in particular? Most codependent relationships revolve around one person's mood or behaviors. If your partner feels upset, then you feel like you must be upset. If your partner wants to go out, then you feel like you need to go out. To act codependently is like giving up your right to make choices. By basing every decision that you make on your partner, you are able to give up on your accountability. It is a way to live just below the radar, but it can also become easy to get placed into a span of unhappiness.

No changes will be enforced until you are able to recognize that certain behavior does need to change. It is okay to admit that your relationship is imperfect; this is the reality. Codependency puts a veil over relationships, causing the individual to believe that their relationship is truly flawless. By ignoring all of the warning signs, you are actually just setting yourself up for failure. A romantic relationship can only thrive on this kind of energy for so long before one or both of you get burnt out. Codependency makes a relationship feel more like work than something enjoyable. In a healthy relationship, both parties involved should feel as though they are getting something beneficial out of it.

Listen to what your loved ones are telling you. It can be hard to open up to the idea of criticism, but when it is coming from someone who truly cares about you, the intention is normally going to be for the best. Hearing an opinion from a third party about how your relationship looks can really help you acknowledge its problems. Someone on the outside is not going to be as biased as you are. When a person who is close to you expresses concern over your behavior or the behavior of your partner, make sure that you give them a chance to explain what they are seeing. The clarity might end up surprising you.

Overall, there is no tell-tale sign that you are in a codependent relationship, but you should be able to get an idea by studying the warnings. Take an honest look at your relation-

AM I CODEPENDENT? AND WHAT DO I DO ABOUT IT?

ships and your own behaviors. There is no need to lie to yourself because this isn't going to fix the problem of being in a relationship with imbalance. Your aim is to correct this by stepping up with your own opinions and viewpoints. You should feel confident enough to freely express your feelings while still being an excellent support system for the person that you are with. A great relationship revolves around mutual caring, so make sure that you are also on the receiving end. It becomes so easy to disregard your own feelings when you are in a codependent situation.

Chapter 4: Codependency with and Without Substance Abuse

It has been stated that codependency originated from those who enable the alcohol addictions of their partners. This is still a very prominent cause of codependency today, creating just as much of a toxic situation as it always has. With any addiction, it becomes dangerous to place yourself in the role of an enabler. No matter how much you love your partner, you should not be encouraging any behavior that they display that actually leads to them using. By letting these things go, you are also enabling them. Not saying anything when they decide to pick up another bottle is just as bad as putting the bottle in their hand. While it is not your role to correct their addiction, it becomes your place to maintain a support system that they can count on. Talking to you should feel like a safe space.

Gambling

ADDICTION CAN BE SEEN in many forms, and alcohol only makes up for a percentage of it. People can be addicted to various things that can still result in a codependent relationship. Gambling is another one, an addiction that starts out small but can generate severe consequences. Even while you're not at a casino, it is so easy to become addicted to gambling because of its accessibility. You can download games on your phone and computer that allow you to gamble with real people and use real money. Someone who develops a gambling addiction might start out with fictitious games at first. These games will serve their purpose, but if the individual has an addictive personality, they will begin to crave more.

This is the point where the person will want gambling to become more real, often deciding to visit a casino or download a more realistic game. Even during this phase, the addiction might not be causing any harm. As a partner to someone who enjoys this, it is natural that you would want to encourage it because it makes your partner happy. A gambling addiction can develop quickly, though. Small bets can turn to large ones, and before you know it, your partner will be making risky decisions that put your welfare at risk. Many people who become seriously addicted to gambling will often lose their assets because of their risky bets.

If you are in a relationship with someone who does this, when do you think you would step in? In a codependent relationship, this point never comes. The individual sits back and allows his or her partner to engage in this risky activity because it appears to make them happy. This isn't always enough, though. Sometimes, we need to be guided toward better choices, especially when we are struggling. This is why addiction can be so deceiving. It can be hard to recognize that your partner is actually struggling inside because of the demeanor that they present externally. They will likely deny that there is a problem at all, potentially even causing you to feel like you are blowing things out of proportion.

Just as alcohol addictions can be treated, there are also programs for gambling addictions. If your partner shows signs of an addictive personality, the best thing that you can do for him or her is to express when their behavior is hurting you. If you stay silent, you are actually enforcing everything that he or she does, even the things that you might not agree with. It is important to speak up about something that you have feelings about, no matter how insignificant it might feel to you. This is how you can avoid falling into patterns of codependency. If you think about it, speaking up is going to benefit both you and your partner. You will find your voice, and they will realize that their actions have consequences.

Sex

THE IDEA OF BEING ADDICTED to sex can seem foreign to some, but it is a real addiction that impacts people on a daily basis. When you are dating someone with this addiction, it can usually manifest in a couple of different ways. You will either find yourself in situations where you are having sex with your partner because you feel that you have to, or you will discover that your partner is cheating on you in order to fuel his or her addiction. A sex addiction is one that should be treated as se-

AM I CODEPENDENT? AND WHAT DO I DO ABOUT IT?

riously as an alcohol or drug addiction. It can become just as damaging and as detrimental. Naturally, more emotions are involved in an addiction like this. If you find that your partner has this problem, it will likely be an instant stab at your self-esteem. You might feel as though you are not good enough to keep your partner in a state of being pleased, or that you are doing something wrong because he or she is never satisfied for long.

You should know that none of this isn't your fault. It wasn't caused by any actions that you have displayed, nor should you make it a point to change anything that you are doing. With any addiction, the only one at fault is the addict. While you should not shame him or her for what they are going through, you also need to make sure that you are protecting yourself in the process. Someone who experiences this type of addiction has a high risk of becoming unfaithful to you. If you find out that this is occurring, but you still stay in the relationship, it can become extremely codependent. Enabling this type of behavior is a way of stating that you place no value on yourself. While it can be extremely difficult to fight the urge to enable your partner, you need to remember that you are worthy of happiness. Make sure that you are standing up for the way that you are being treated. If you don't, you can guarantee that your partner is going to do this again. Addiction takes away logic most of the time. You can't expect your partner to just "get better." In order to heal, it takes effort and the desire to change. This is something that you can't force; your partner has to be willing to change.

Food

JUST AS EASILY AS ANYTHING else can become an addictive behavior, so can eating. Most of us do not see food as a "danger," but it can develop into something that takes over our lives. Individuals who experience food addiction might end up craving food after they have already eaten. They also tend to overeat, even after they have eaten enough to feel full. By acting on excessive eating, the individual tends to become overwhelmed with guilt. This can really bring a person down, resulting in destructive behavior. When you feel bad about yourself, you might withdraw from other people and from activities that you normally enjoy. The person might end up making excuses for their eating habits, acting in disbelief that there is any problem. Depression will commonly develop if the disorder is not acknowledged.

Codependency can definitely happen within a relationship that involves food addiction. The person suffering from the addiction is already going to be having a major struggle with willpower on a daily basis, so this puts them in a rather vulnerable state. Even if they do not outwardly express this, the shame and guilt are going to be affecting them internally. A codependent partner might ignore or brush off the food addiction, and therefore enable the overeating or other related behaviors. Not only will this result in the addict feeling down, but it can also lead to health problems. The codependent individual might deny that there is a problem altogether; therefore, keeping up the sense of denial that will prevent their partner from seeking help.

Having a food addiction can also be known as having a binge eating disorder. It is a serious condition that greatly benefits from having the help of a professional to overcome it. Being with a partner that chooses to ignore the fact that you are struggling is only going to make the addiction worse. Your partner should be your voice of reason and your support system, but if they are codependent, this isn't going to be the case. They are going to cling to the destructive individual, probably feeling a sense of security in knowing that they are close to this person. The one suffering from addiction will use the codependent individual as a crutch, often believing that things are going to be okay and that the behavior should continue. Just with any other codependent relationship, the two individuals encourage the same patterns of behavior over and over again. It can become a vicious cycle.

Shopping

HAVING A SHOPPING ADDICTION can be similar to having a gambling addiction; both revolve around spending money. To a shopping addict, the feeling that they normally become addicted to is the actual thrill of spending money. From clothes to home decor, anything that can be purchased is easily able to become part of the thrill. The act can be done either in person or online, giving the individual many options to choose from. Shopping becomes somewhat of a game in itself, providing the one who is addicted to it with so many chances to spend their money. Shopping addicts might hide their behavior, paying for things with cash or using secret accounts in order to disguise the problem from their partners. It is when the partner knows what is going on, but does not do anything to help, that the relationship can turn codependent very easily.

When someone acts as an enabler to a shopping addict, they might brush off the seriousness of the issue. They might even be willing to give the person money in order for them to continue shopping without realizing what negative impacts this can make. The more that you fuel any addiction, the worse that it is going to become. To a shopping addict, making a purchase is never going to feel satisfying. They are going to have to keep doing it repeatedly to feel any sense of temporary bliss. It is a short-lived feeling, though. Because the act of shopping is likely happening in order to fill some type of void, the individual is never going to find exactly what he or she is looking for. He or she might rely on the behavior to make themselves feel better or to distract them from other problems in life. This can form a very isolating pattern with some grave consequences.

Work

SOME OF US ARE VERY career-oriented, and that is normally seen as something that is admirable. Being good at your job and staying devoted to it can create some excellent behavioral traits. Just like anything else though, too much of something can lead to an addiction with real consequences. When someone is addicted to working, they will choose their job over anything. This includes family, friends, and other obligations that the person might have. These individuals can have a priority over work that is so strong, they do not even consider the damage that is being done to the other relationships around them. Because they find something thrilling about working and satisfactory in success, the individual will not want to lose sight of this. They would be willing to turn their backs on things that were once important if it meant that they could work. Even when at home, the individual will likely be focusing on work, trying to see if anything else can be done until they go back.

It can be extremely difficult to date someone who is addicted to their job. For one, you are sacrificing the attention that you deserve. The individual isn't going to be able to tend to your needs because he or she is going to be so focused on the tasks at work. By standing back and allowing this to happen, insisting that you are still being treated fairly, you are being an enabler. The codependent individual might even praise the person for being so focused on work, and this will fuel the addiction. People can lose a lot when they are suffering in this way. Connections that were once strong can crumble to nothing. Because there is no time to care about other people, the individual will often lose the support of other family and friends around them. This will make the codependent individual feel even more important, showing them that they are the only one in the addicted individual's life who is allowed to stay close. Even when they aren't being treated fairly, they will still see this as a special privilege.

Chapter 5: Childhood: Developmental Conditions Contributing to Codependency

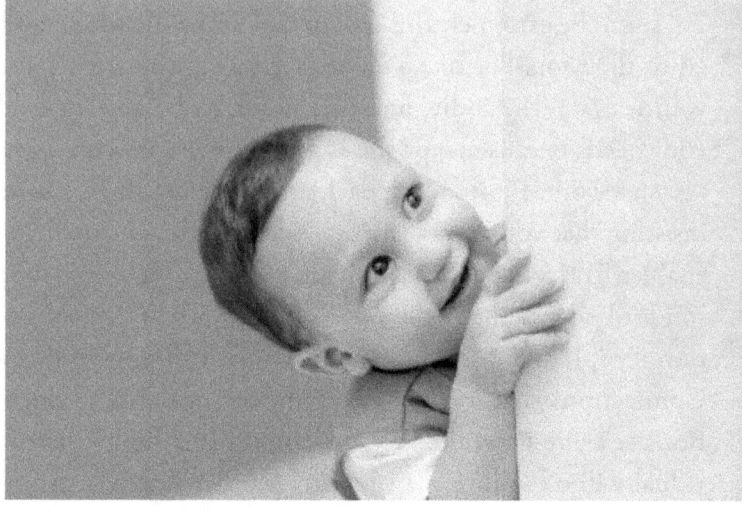

As you are learning, codependency is a very challenging way to live. Those who grow up to become codependent were normally exposed to situations in their childhood that lead them to these actions. Psychologists state that there is a clear connection between our upbringing and the way that we develop as adults. For this reason, growing up in a home that is unstable or has some sort of codependent element is only going to show the child that this is how he or she should act. Children learn by example, and they can be very impressionable. The following are examples of situations experienced in childhood that could lead to codependent behavior in the future:

AM I CODEPENDENT? AND WHAT DO I DO ABOUT IT?

- **Having an Addict as a Parent**: For several reasons, growing up in a household with a parent who has an addiction has the ability to be very damaging to a child. Not only is there a possibility for neglect and a loss of innocence, but there is also a chance to learn how to be codependent. If a child sees that one parent is an addict and the other is codependent, this is going to appear normal. The child will learn that this is how addiction should be treated and will likely mimic these behaviors if they are ever in this type of situation. Aside from impacting their behavioral responses, it can also lead them into a pattern of seeking out those who are struggling with addiction. A child who grew up to learn codependency might gravitate toward those who are "damaged." It is going to be in their nature to want to fix the problem, even when they are actually only enabling it.

- **Growing Up in a Big Family**: It can be easy to get lost in a family that is made up of several members. If you grew up with a lot of siblings, there is a chance that you have felt forgotten or ignored at some point in time. Prolonged experiences like this can lead a child to believe that they are not as important as other people. When this child grows up, he or she will feel like it is their job to put others first. While this can be a great quality within a reasonable amount, it can also lead to self-destructive behavior. Those who have no regard for their own feelings can often find themselves in situations that they feel "stuck" in. Because there is such a lack of motivation to change the situation, the individual will stay put because it is familiar and safe. The thought of being treated better isn't going to be enough to create a lasting change. They might promise to leave, but they will find themselves unable to because of the conditioning that they received in their childhood, telling them that they should always come last.

- **Being a Mature Child**: Some children do not get to experience the magic of childhood before they learn how to care for a household. In some situations, a child is forced to mature early due to having parents who cannot care for themselves or siblings that made to be their responsibility. This is damaging to a child because the sense of wonder and excitement quickly fades away. When parents are incapable of caring for themselves or another child, the individual has a huge responsibility placed onto them. They are now being made to take on a role that they never should have needed to take on. This is a very mature role to fill for a child that is still trying to figure out who she or he is and how the world works. This can lead to many skewed viewpoints about the world and a lot of confusion when it comes to interacting with other people. This child is going to grow up feeling like he or she is responsible for all of the bad things that happen, and they are going to feel the need to fix them.

AM I CODEPENDENT? AND WHAT DO I DO ABOUT IT?

- **Having Trouble Saying No**: Some children are conditioned to feel that their right to say no means that they do not love their parents. They grow up believing that if they choose to say no, they are directly disappointing their parents. Children aim to please those who raise them. This is a very detrimental behavioral pattern to fall into because it creates a lot of problems going into adulthood. A child who grew up like this might find themselves in an abusive relationship, unable to leave because he or she is too scared to say no. Taking away a child's voice like this is one of the most detrimental actions that can be done by the parents. Because the child feels so uncertain about self-expression, he or she will never fully be able to feel comfortable with who they are as a person. Instead, they are going to try and mold themselves into what is ideal for other people around them. This sense of validation is going to be the only thing that allows him or her to feel secure in who they are.

- **Not Being Good Enough**: Validation is essential in childhood. It teaches us that we are capable of so much, and it motivates us to live happily and excitedly. A child who does not receive enough praise is going to feel like they are not good enough. This might also come to develop when a child is being forced to live in the shadow of his or her siblings. When you feel like you are not good enough in your childhood, this will cause you to grow up with a strong sense of insecurity. You might feel too scared to go after the things that you really want in life because of your fear of failure. Children who grew up this way are not at fault for their behavior as adults. It is a parent's job to make sure that their child feels secure and loved. When you do not receive this affirmative action, it is impossible to tell if what you are doing is right or wrong. A child might even begin to rebel in order to gain attention. When this situation goes unnoticed, it can become a definite cause for codependency in the future.

- **Not Being Allowed to Cry**: As a human being, crying can be a very healthy and therapeutic response to the things that make us emotionally overwhelmed. It can act as a release and a way for us to reset ourselves. Some children are scolded by their parents for crying which can lead them to believe that it is never okay to cry. As a child, many things are going to feel confusing and difficult. Crying is natural and being fed a narrative that crying is a bad thing is going to only lead to emotional suppression. A person who wasn't allowed to cry as a child will likely have trouble with opening up as an adult. Since they were made to suppress their problems, they are likely not going to be willing to discuss them with other people. This can cause a person to live in pain or in less than ideal circumstances for extended amounts of time. Behavior like this has the ability to lead someone into a deep depression because they will feel like no one understands them. Being in a codependent relationship becomes an answer because the other person is usually too deep into their own issues to question the individual about their emotions. They can both exist within their negative habits without having to acknowledge any of the deeper underlying issues.

- **Thinking That People Cannot Be Trusted**: When dealing with a person whose childhood included parents with instabilities, a child will feel like they cannot form trust. If the parents are using love as a bargaining chip, the child is going to feel like things can change at any given moment because they are so unstable. A child needs routine and consistency, and this is not usually possible in a household that includes addicts. The life of an addict is naturally going to be unpredictable, and this will end up impacting the child as well. When the child grows up, they are going to remember that their first impression of trust has been shattered. Maybe they have never felt a true bond of trust before. For this reason, trust issues are prominent. It might be very hard to put this person at ease because he or she believes that everyone they dates is going to withdraw their love the same way his or her parents did. It is a very damaging cycle and a very unhappy way to live.

- **Feeling Like No One Cares**: Children who grow up in a household where they are mainly ignored will begin to believe that no one cares about them. This places a dangerous sense of carelessness into their heads. Those who grow into adulthood might continue to believe that no one truly cares. No matter what words are said or what actions are taken, the individual might still believe that they are less worthy than other people. If depression is combined with this worthless state of mind, then suicide is definitely something that is likely to be considered. It is a very detrimental way for a child to grow up, and it can also create a large sense of loneliness. A child needs endless amounts of support as they grow up. Even when others display true caring actions, the individual isn't going to be willing to believe that the other person really cares. The need for codependency can grow because the individual might enjoy having control over their partner. They might feel that, because they can control their relationship, they will make sure that their partner never leaves them.

All of the examples given are contributing factors when it comes to codependency. Because children are very impressionable, their upbringing certainly has a lot to do with how their behavior develops into adulthood. If a child is presented with an environment where he is left to fend for himself and sort through his own feelings, codependency is definitely likely to follow. Those who aren't nurtured at a young age often feel that they need to protect themselves until they can find somebody to latch onto. This is when the codependency begins. Breaking these patterns can be very hard because they have been occurring since childhood.

Codependency can be defined as a learned behavior. Though it is possible to learn, it is harder to untrain yourself to display these traits. Codependency eventually becomes a lifestyle, and you will find that people who suffer from it will deny that they are suffering at all. Without a true sense of identity, it is natural that a child is going to learn everything they need to know from their parental figures. It makes sense that parents who are deep into addictions or other negative behaviors are not going to be able to provide the examples needed for their children. They are going to be less able to provide guidance and life lessons. Instead, the child is just going to observe that they must be the one to step in and take care of the parent.

While childhood developmental issues aren't the only factor when it comes to codependency, they do have a very strong influence. It can be hard to understand why an adult is codependent if you do not know about their childhood upbringing. This is why it is impossible to assume that someone can simply stop acting in a codependent manner at any time that they choose. The behavior becomes such a part of them that they do not know how to survive without it. This is especially true if it has been a lifestyle since childhood. Someone who has been codependent for such a long time is also prone to self-confidence issues. They might feel too insecure to make their own choices or step out of their comfort zone because all they have ever known is the caretaker role, even as a child.

In order to avoid this kind of upbringing, it is essential that the child has a loving home environment. Whether they have one guardian or more than one guardian, a positive example is a necessity. There are warning signs to look out for in children. Some of them include low self-esteem, extreme worry, placing blame on oneself, lack of trust, fear of being alone, and difficulty making decisions. If a child begins to display any kind of these behaviors, there is a chance that codependency is forming. Luckily, if it is noticed quick enough, a professional will be able to help the child build his or her confidence back up.

Chapter 6: The One Root Cause of Codependency

Taking a look at the deepest reason for the development of codependent behavior, it can be seen that its development requires more than a difficult upbringing or neglectful parenting. The first thing that people normally perceive about codependent individuals is that they want to take control over other people "for their own good." While there is some truth behind this, the real reason for the cause of codependency is much deeper. Codependent individuals do love to try and help people in order to make their lives better or easier. Because of this desire, they are very giving people who would not hesitate to go through great lengths to help. This becomes damaging because they do not have much regard for their own feelings or desires.

Afraid to discourage their partner in any way, a codependent individual is going to be the first one to offer support, even when they do not necessarily agree with the destructive behavior. They want to be known for always being there for the other person. Filling that role provides them with a true sense of purpose that they might have never felt in their childhood. While having a purpose is a great way to live, there must be a balance behind the desire. Choosing to solely serve another person is only going to lead the individual down a harmful path of bad habits. From putting up with abuse to never having needs met, a codependent individual is not the type of person who would be considered a "go-getter."

The true cause of codependent behavior derives from a need for a particular kind of fulfillment. This fulfillment does not come from standard behaviors such as maintaining a successful career or owning a beautiful home. Instead, a codependent individual seeks out fulfillment through other people. This is where the term becomes so relevant. The individual seeks these sources in a way that is similar to an addict. The person that they attach themselves to becomes their crutch. They would do anything for that person, and they feel satisfaction when they can receive approval from that person. In a way, it is as though they become addicted themselves.

Because of unresolved pain or something that makes the person feel uncomfortable with who they are, they decide to medicate by receiving attention from the person that they latch on to. The pain is never addressed or dealt with; hence the individual is stuck in the same type of behavioral patterns for a long time. A codependent individual is unlikely to realize that there is even pain stored deep down until it is brought to their attention. It is usually suppressed to the point where it just becomes numb and forgotten about until triggered. The mutual dependency makes the individual feel as though their problems are being solved when in reality, they are just being pushed aside until the next one arises.

Where Does the Pain Come From?

THE CONCEPT OF HOW codependency happens is a fairly easy one to understand. The complex part lies behind the cause of the pain. A traumatic event is something that can cause a person to shut down when it comes to addressing pain or emotional turmoil. Trauma has the ability to numb a person enough that they do not even feel they need help to get through it. Any event like this that is experienced but never properly dealt with can lead to codependency. As the pain is being suppressed, the codependent behavior takes over more and more. Soon, the individual will tune out the trauma and become entirely focused on the individual that they are attached to. Understandably, this puts a lot of pressure on a romantic partner. The relationship can become very intense very quickly because both parties need each other to fill certain emotional voids. Instead of working through the issues together, they are ignored and replaced with other feelings.

A person can also experience pain from a steady pattern of codependent relationships. Even if there were no codependency issues in childhood, a person who has previously engaged in a codependent relationship is likely to do it again. As mentioned, it isn't something that can be easily unlearned. Getting rid of these behavioral patterns takes a lot of effort and patience. The individual has to gain a whole new sense of trust in themselves in order to feel independently secure. Because this tends to be the pattern, the codependent individual might begin to believe that they are the problem. They might feel as though people treat them a certain way because of something that they are doing which is why they seldom choose to speak up if there is any wrongdoing. It is almost as if they believe that they deserve to be treated poorly.

Anything that has the ability to cause us pain can become detrimental if not addressed. All forms of emotional pain are very valid reasons for why we can develop certain conditions. In order to better handle pain management, the help of a professional is always recommended. Because we all have gone through different situations, a professional is going to be able to pinpoint exactly what it is that is being held on to. Generally speaking, being open can also help with pain management. The willingness to express what causes us discomfort is a lot better than holding it inside to eventually become suppressed. By practicing healthy techniques in order to deal with things that are painful, there is less of a chance that you will become codependent.

How Good Turns Bad

THE CONCEPT OF CODEPENDENCY can sound minor at first. It is an individual who just wants to help their partner succeed and who cares about their partner's happiness. These are great qualities to have, but what is important is moderation. No matter how much good intention is behind each action, it still has the ability to become destructive. When a person becomes so concerned with making someone else happy, they disregard their own feelings and emotions. Nobody is able to live this way and remain mentally balanced. The more that it becomes a struggle to manage their own life, the more that the person will actually insert themselves into the other person's life. It is a major act of avoidance on all levels of everything that has to do with their own personal struggles.

Even though a codependent individual has these great qualities, the way that they are utilized creates a negative outcome. Not only do they lose touch with their own personal needs, but they also push other people in their lives away because they are so focused on one individual. A codependent individual will have a hard time keeping friendships afloat because they will not have the time or effort to devote to them. Their partner is their main priority, and if anything gets in the way of being there for their partner, they aren't going to do it. An example is someone turning down a friend who wants to go to lunch because their partner will be home. Instead of having fun by catching up with a friend like the person truly wants to do, they will opt for staying home to be with their partner.

Codependency can cause rifts with family, too. The individual isn't going to take advice or suggestions when their family decides to step in and help. This act is going to seem intrusive to the codependent individual. Instead, they will likely push their family away and become even more closed off. Trying to help a person who cannot see that they are doing something wrong is difficult and frustrating. It can often seem like nothing is getting through to the person and that their ways will never change. The important thing is not to force the individual into changing their behavior. This is only going to create more resistance.

Through the Eyes of Codependency

TO A PERSON SUFFERING from codependency, they behave in this way because they want to help. They believe that helping their partner is going to solve all of his or her problems. Codependency causes an individual to believe that they are solely responsible for taking on this task. This is a pattern that might be mimicked from earlier life experiences. When someone tries to get the codependent individual to act more independently, the individual sees this as a betrayal to their partner. Their worst fear is disappointing them or not being able to help them, so doing something that is self-focused is just going to feel wrong to them.

When it comes to public struggles, a codependent individual will take on any and all burdens in order to make it appear that everything is externally harmonious. They do not enjoy vulnerability, and they will go to great lengths to keep up this illusion for their partner. Image is a very important aspect of a codependent relationship. Because the destructive individual cannot control certain impulses, this gives the codependent individual a lot of damage control that must be done. This can be anything from lying about situations to making excuses for their partner. They will do anything that they can to turn the attention away from any imperfection or struggle that is occurring.

It is the opinion of the codependent individual that their partner will not be able to function without them. Not only does this give them a great sense of purpose, but it also encourages the partner to hold onto them just as much as they are holding on. This strengthens the bond between the two, creating a comfortable lifestyle. It might not make much sense to onlookers who get a glimpse into the way that they operate, but it will feel entirely natural to them. Each person has a purpose, one getting to act on their addiction or destructive behavior and the other enabling these actions. This will continue on until something with a heavy influence causes it to stop. It is highly unlikely for either of the individuals to have a change in behavior once they are already so used to a codependent lifestyle.

Future Impacts

CONSIDER A CODEPENDENT relationship, and then imagine that couple starting a family. Naturally, the children are going to grow up being exposed to this damaging behavior while thinking that it is entirely normal. This is when the cycle can start all over again, influencing their children to the point where they also become codependent adults. The impacts of codependency are sometimes far greater than they seem. What appears to be a slightly dysfunctional relationship can evolve into the example that a child sees as they grow up. Most of the time, the parents will be so wrapped up in their codependent behavior that they will not even realize how much of an impact it is having on their children.

Very observant and keen to examples, children are going to pick up on the behavior quickly. This is why awareness of the issue is super important. If you feel like you are in a codependent relationship, you need to consider all implications (past, present, and future). Just because something does not directly impact other people does not mean that it isn't making an impression. It is also incredibly important to reevaluate your self-worth. You need to believe that you are just as worthy of a happy life as your partner, or anyone else. Codependency takes away a lot of the best freedoms that there are to experience in life, and it is unfair for anyone to have to live that way. Telling someone that you trust when you think you are in this situation is a great first step to breaking the cycle.

Another way for you to think about the impacts of your codependent relationship can be by focusing on your own mental health. Prolonged behavior that tears you down is only going to make you feel bad mentally. While you can try to push these feelings away, you are likely going to be met with them when they are triggered in the future. When you become so used to living in a codependent relationship, you might be missing out on other wonderful opportunities. A codependent lifestyle does not allow for much personal growth. Because things stay the same for such a long time, the individual will normally not have any desire to do anything else, even when presented with the opportunity to do so.

It can be easy to forget that your mental health is important. Without it, you are not going to be able to function.

AM I CODEPENDENT? AND WHAT DO I DO ABOUT IT?

Things like going to work and caring for your family become exhausting when you are not mentally prepared to take on each role. We all need a break sometimes, and this is especially true for codependent individuals. If you are able to set aside the time to take care of yourself, you might be able to remember that you are also a priority in your own life. Your well-being matters just as much as your partner's. There is an underrated joy in being able to do the things that you want to do, so try to give yourself these moments whenever you can.

Chapter 7: Why Codependency Can Easily Lead to Abuse

AM I CODEPENDENT? AND WHAT DO I DO ABOUT IT?

Codependency is a fear-based condition that causes a lot of conflicting feelings. Those who wish to live for their partners will often do so until it becomes miserable, and then they will fear what will happen if they were to leave. This can stem from a fear of abandonment, or maybe even a fear for their own well-being. There is also the possibility that the individual has a fear of being alone or being uncomfortable. These are all understandable roadblocks on the path toward living a healthy life. It is incredibly easy for a codependent relationship to turn into an abusive relationship because of this lingering fear. An individual will put up with endless abuse if it means that they will feel secure or not alone. It can often feel as though they are stuck between a rock and a hard place because, deep down, they are still unhappy.

Taking a close look at the dynamic of a codependent relationship, it is easy to see who has the upper hand. The partner in the relationship seemingly has nothing to worry about. He or she is going to act the way that they want, and if necessary, they will force their partner to stay by using fear tactics or worse. This method tends to work so well on codependent individuals because it gives them the purpose that they consistently crave. Even though they aren't being treated fairly in return, they will see the relationship as the best that they are able to get and that they should feel grateful for it. This low sense of self-worth becomes very hindering to the individual.

To someone seeing the relationship on the outside, it might not make any sense. You might know someone who is in an abusive relationship like this, and you will probably wonder why they just don't pack up and leave. It isn't usually this simple. When emotions are involved, the abuser has a lot of control. Not only can they use fear to make their partner stay, but they can also prey on their weaknesses. For example, if a codependent individual needs to feel important in order to be happy, their partner will express that they are important after abuse occurs. This sends a confusing message to the individual, but it is usually going to be enough to make them stay. They will start to see this treatment as normal, often making up excuses for their partner's behavior if they are approached about the situation.

As we know, a codependent individual would go to great lengths to protect the reputation of their partner. They would be willing to lie and come up with excuses when other people begin to question the dynamic. In their mind, they deserve this treatment and they might even feel lucky to have any of this attention at all. When their partner completes a task that is of the bare minimum, the codependent individual will likely take that as a sign that their partner truly cares about them. They will feel as though this small act of kindness is enough to make up for the countless moments of abuse and unfair treatment. It can become a devastating cycle because the individual will truly believe that there is nothing wrong with the way that they are being treated, therefore never having the desire to change their current situation.

Some people feel like it is just easier to stay, even when they know they are being treated badly. In codependency, the individual will likely see the relationship as something that is worth being part of because it is better than being alone. Most people in this mindset will have some sort of fear that is either rooted in abandonment or loneliness. They would rather be unhappy in a relationship with someone that does not have their best interest at heart than being single and working on their own personal growth. This thought might happen subconsciously as the individual struggles through dealing with their partner. They might consider leaving several times, but they will normally not have the capacity to follow through because of the fear that they have inside.

Of course, sometimes this fear has nothing to do with abandonment. If the relationship is toxic enough, the individual might be in genuine fear for their own life. Having an abusive partner is an extremely difficult experience, and it is one that takes a careful strategy to remove yourself from. Those who go against their abusive partners might have to face physical and verbal repercussions. This can be so traumatizing that the person will often just give up and think that putting up with the abuse is better than what might happen if they try to leave. If you or someone you know is going through this, feeling helpless can be devastating. While it is important to be careful with a situation like this, telling someone that you trust is going to be the first step toward getting help. No one is going to know about how bad the situation truly is unless you tell them.

Control

AN ABUSER MIGHT BE fully capable of showing their partner love at times, but the need for control overshadows this. Because a codependent relationship is already skewed when it comes to balance, the abuser is going to use this to his or her advantage. He or she will have no problem taking control over the other person and asking for all of their needs to be met while giving nothing back in return. The more that the codependent individual is willing to comply, the higher the chance that the pattern is just going to continue until it becomes worse and worse. The two people end up feeding off of one another's energy because the codependent individual has the tendency to relinquish control. When there is such a shift in power, the abuser is going to take this as a signal to keep doing what they want to do.

Normally, codependent individuals enjoy giving up their control. They hate to make decisions because it can feel too overwhelming. Instead of thinking for themselves and what choices they need to make, they would rather put all of their energy into their partner's needs. This can seem like a better option to the individual at first, but once they start getting taken advantage of, they are going to want out of the situation without knowing how to get out. Once the relationship has progressed to this point, it becomes so difficult to leave because the codependent individual cannot see a life without their partner. The thought of living for themselves and making their own decisions can appear worse than being controlled. It is an unfortunate cycle that occurs more often than you might think.

A person can go a very long time while being controlled by someone else. Once all of their defenses are dropped and their desire to live independently fades away, the person becomes entirely submissive to their partner. Any warnings or actions that protest what is happening in the relationship eventually become suppressed and then forgotten. They don't stay away forever though. When you suppress any strong emotion, it is bound to come back twice as strong when you least expect it. Certain behavior that is repeated at the hands of an abuser can be enough to trigger the feelings and send the codependent individual in a downward spiral. This becomes one of those ruts that seems impossible to escape from.

Narcissism

A NARCISSISTIC PERSONALITY can appear in someone who is abusive. Narcissists believe that only their own desires matter, and they will stop at nothing to get what they want, even if it means hurting other people. Dealing with narcissism in a codependent relationship is fairly common. To recognize a narcissist, you will probably encounter some of these traits:

- **Lack of Empathy**: A person who does not have any empathy will not feel bad when they see another person struggling. They will also have no problem with putting people that they care about into situations that cause them to struggle. There is no guilt or sadness when it comes to a narcissistic individual, only personal gain. They are always looking to see how they can get ahead, and it does not matter who they have to hurt along the way.

- **Need for Praise**: A narcissist is going to love attention. If you give them a compliment, they are going to want more. Nothing is ever satisfactory enough, so you will likely find that a narcissist is going to do whatever it takes in order for you to give them praises. Being with a partner like this can be very exhausting because you become so worn down in order to make your partner feel good, while you are unhappy.

- **Exploiting with Shame**: Leave it to a narcissist to make you feel bad about the things that you are already self-conscious about. A narcissistic partner will have no trouble with using shame in order to get you to do what he or she wants. They might put your love into question, implying that if you do not do what they want, then you do not truly love them. This is very damaging behavior, and a codependent individual is likely going to comply by nature.

- **Living in a Fantasy**: The life that a narcissistic individual lives is one that is far from reality. He or she might believe something so much to the point where they force their partner to believe it too. There is no right or wrong when it comes to dealing with a narcissist, so there is no use in trying to argue by using morals. They are going to believe exactly what they need to believe in order for it to fit their narrative.

- **Bullying and Belittling**: If a narcissist isn't getting what he or she wants, you will find that they have no problem using tactics like bullying in order to get their point across. They will make you feel so bad about yourself that you will feel that your needs are less important, maybe not important at all. This personality type is very strong, and it can be nearly impossible for a codependent individual to stand up to someone like this because they are naturally going to be coming from a submissive stance. The belittling will be putting them down just enough to make them believe that they would not be able to live without this person. If they were to leave this person, they would likely feel lost and confused.

If you feel you may have been or are currently being affected by a narcissist, you may be interested in my companion book on the subject titled, "Invisible Abuse," by myself, Kara Lawrence. This book dives deeper into the covert tactics that narcissists use to manipulate and abuse, and can be very hard to spot without the proper information at hand.

Past Abuse

THOSE WITH A HISTORY of abuse have a strong likelihood of becoming involved in a codependent relationship. This revolves around the desire to be needed. A codependent individual just wants to be good enough for his or her partner, and they are willing to go out of their way to prove this to them. Defining their worth based on the response that they get from their partner, the codependent person will keep trying to do whatever it takes to keep them satisfied. Because of abuse that happened in the past, a fear of this happening again is usually prominent. The individual will try to make themselves as agreeable as they can, willing to make huge sacrifices for the other person if it means that it will make their life easier.

A lot of people who have experienced abuse in the past will often take on a strong need to control every aspect of their lives in order to avoid being abused again. They might be very particular over the way that they do things because they do not want to be hurt again. This is where a codependent relationship can trick the individual because it takes control away from them and allows the partner to take over. Their partner is usually someone who is fairly charismatic, convincing the person that they are important and will be taken care of. As the comfort level grows, the control is then passed on so that the relationship becomes codependent.

Once this happens, the codependent individual will no longer trust themselves. Instead, all of the trust is placed in their partner. It is up to the partner to guide both of them toward what he or she believes is best. Because they can appear so confident externally, it is normally very easy to accept what he or she is saying as the truth. It is as though both people take on one personality, and they learn how to operate by one taking control and the other giving in to this control. Understandably, this is not a healthy lifestyle. It is never a good idea to place all of your control into the hands of another. In order to engage in a healthy relationship, balance is necessary for both parties' happiness.

Chapter 8: Psychology of Being Controlling: When the Abused Becomes Abusive

Anxiety is a prominent feeling to a codependent individual. As discussed, there can often be a fear of abandonment within the relationship. If there is enough of this fear present, someone who is being controlled can actually switch roles and become controlling. It is a learned behavior that the individual has plenty of experience with since it is presently happening to them. Being in a codependent relationship is an agreement to relinquish your control to your partner. You will normally not have any decision-making factors in the relationship, and you will be living each day according to what your partner feels is right. The switch can happen at any moment. Enough of certain negative treatment can trigger a response when you least expect it. A person who is mostly submissive will snap, and then they will have the need to control the dynamic of the relationship.

This can be displayed in several ways, but each action is going to suggest that the individual is taking control of their partner. From manipulating him or her to stay home that you can be together or controlling who they get to spend time with outside of your relationship, are ways that the roles can be reversed. During this desire to control, there is normally no ill intention behind it. In fact, the individual will see it as the exact opposite—they will want to do this solely because they feel like this is what will benefit the relationship. We all know that codependency is unhealthy and can cause some intense feelings, so the individual's desire to control the situation is stemming from this need to be with their partner. Certain things will feel as though they are not good enough. The codependent individual is going to crave more; therefore, they will choose controlling actions in order to get more of their partner.

Sides of Abuse

ABUSIVE RELATIONSHIPS can differ so greatly from one another, even though they are all unhealthy and display behavior that is greatly hindering to the people involved. Within a codependent relationship, the dynamic of the abuse can be interesting. While one person is destructive and careless with his or her actions, they are normally not striving for manipulation tactics. Instead, they simply do exactly what they want to do, and the codependent partner chooses to stick around. While the weight of their decisions does make it easy for the partner to want to stay, it is ultimately the codependent individual's own choice. They will stand by their partner, even if it means that they are the last priority and being treated unfairly. This is made very apparent from the beginning, though. A destructive individual does not have time to create false pretenses. He or she is going to act in their own pattern of toxic behavior, and this is not likely going to change by the influence of his or her partner. Knowing this, the codependent individual still decides to stay in the relationship, even when it is filled with unhappiness.

A certain dynamic can appear once the two become comfortable with one another. As the destructive individual is on his or her own path to doing exactly what they want, the codependent individual might feel the need to reel them in. This begins the controlling efforts. It is a very two-sided controlling relationship, believe it or not. The main difference between the two sets of behavior is that the former is unapologetic about his or her destructive behavior, while the codependent feels so uncomfortable that this results in the need to take control and manipulate the relationship to their liking. Not all codependent relationships see this kind of abuse, but it is something that is highly likely to happen over time. This person is going to see that they aren't getting their basic needs met, yet they still will not want to leave their partner. Therefore, the only logical solution in their mind is to try to take control of their partner.

Imaginably, this does not always turn out as planned. A person who is very rooted in his or her ways is going to be stubborn. They aren't going to succumb easily to any type of outside influence, even if it is manipulation. This is when the relationship can turn very toxic. If he or she finds out that they are being controlled, the backlash can be expected. The dynamic within the relationship can turn out to be incredibly tumultuous, yet neither party is going to back down. Because this is the life that they both know so well, they aren't going to be considering other options. People will live this way for years at a time, destroying their bond and any self-worth that remains. Instead of reasonably parting ways, the addiction to stay together is much stronger. It might take a huge, life-altering event to show them that they do not belong together. There is very little reasoning with people who are in a relationship with this dynamic. Only they can decide when they are done engaging in such a relationship.

Empath/Narcissist Abuse

IN ORDER TO COMPARE two different situations, consider the type of abuse that occurs within a relationship of an empath and a narcissist. This abuse is one-sided, giving a clear distinction between the abuser (the narcissist) and the victim (the empath). Because an empath is rooted in compassion, it is easy for one to become overtaken by someone with a strong narcissistic personality. The two are opposites when it comes to personality types. A narcissist is someone who chooses to live for themselves, no matter what it takes. He or she does not consider the feelings of other people or the impact that their behavior will make. Instead, they focus on what they can do in order to get themselves ahead. There is no empathy involved in their decision-making process because they cannot feel empathy. For this reason, it becomes easy and almost natural to abuse their partner. In their mind, they are simply trying to get what they want. The feelings of their partner aren't going to matter to them.

This creates an incredible rift in the relationship, causing the empath to feel like they might actually deserve this treatment. They aren't going to speak up against their abuser, even if it is their partner because this is against their nature. Instead, an empath would be sooner to justify their partner's actions. They might even trick themselves into believing that they deserve the abuse because of something that they have done. Self-worth is incredibly difficult to maintain when you are being controlled and manipulated. Because an empath is such an impressionable personality type, the narcissist has a great advantage. It becomes effortless to control their partner, and they enjoy every minute of it. This is a pattern that is incredibly difficult to break, often because the submissive individual will fear to leave her partner. The fear can stem from losing the relationship, or even from receiving worse abuse as an outcome. It is a very dangerous situation to become a part of.

Manipulation Tactics

IF YOU FEEL LIKE YOU are in an abusive relationship, no matter who is responsible for the abusive, consider if there are displays of manipulation tactics. They can be easy to miss if you are not looking for them. Here are some of the most commonly seen tactics within abusive codependent relationships:

- **The Home Advantage**: A controlling individual might be in agreement when the other party suggests that the behavior needs to be discussed. A way that they can manipulate this to their advantage is by only talking about the issue in a place where they are still going to have the upper-hand. For example, they might suggest a meeting place that is their own domain (their office or their car) in order to maintain a position of control. From the start, this isn't going to fix any of the imbalance because it is still being discussed in a way that is maintaining the imbalance. When important issues need to be discussed, it is essential that each person feels as though they are starting off on the same page.

- **First Words**: Despite any controlling nature, a manipulative individual will usually allow their partner to speak first. While this comes across as a genuine desire to hear what the other person has to say, they will actually use this to their advantage. By being able to hear the other party speak, they will be able to dissect the statement and find any flaws or weaknesses within it. This makes the other person feel important and heard at first, but they will soon realize that they are still being controlled in some way.

- **Intellectual Bullying**: This tactic occurs when a person tries to overload their partner with facts and statistics in order to bully them into submission. They will often speak so confidently about the issue that the other person becomes intimidated. Most of the time, their argument isn't even actually making any sense. All of the noise is being directed at their partner in the hopes that they will become so overwhelmed that they simply give in. This is the outcome a lot of the time.

- **Raised Voices**: Leave it to a manipulative individual to use yelling as a manipulation tactic. To an abuser, being louder means that they have control over the situation. It is a way to maintain power over the other person, no matter what is being said. Name-calling can also come into play here. The abuser is going to do whatever it takes in order to overpower the other person. If they do not have an argument to push, then they will likely resort to language that is meant to be overpowering and intimidating.

- **Immediate Decisions**: A manipulative individual will not give you time to think about your choices. Instead, he or she is going to want the answer right away, therefore putting an immense amount of pressure onto his or her partner. These individuals demand decisions, unfairly placing the burden of stress onto the other person when they maintain a neutral stance. By placing all of the blame onto the other person, the manipulative individual will then try to make them do all of the work in order to make the situation better. Taking a look at this, you can see that they still aren't claiming responsibility for any of the hardships.

- **Silence as a Weapon**: One of the most passive-aggressive behaviors that an abuser can display is the silent treatment. Being ignored is an extremely negative response to receive from a partner who is supposed to care about you. This becomes especially true when you are trying to work through important issues. An abuser isn't going to care about his or her partner's feelings. When he or she is done talking, or when they want their partner to suffer, they will simply give them the silent treatment until their partner is begging them to talk to them. This is a huge misuse of power, as you can see. It really has the ability to tear a person down in a major way.

Detachment

HEARING ABOUT ALL OF these dangers regarding abusive relationships, you might be wondering if it is even possible to get out of one. The answer is yes, and detachment is the key. Being able to detach yourself from a person who is no good for you is ultimately the only way that you are going to be able to make progress. Because codependency forms a tight bond between two people, even though it is unhealthy, it can take some time to let this go. The point of being codependent is because the two of you are comfortable with one another. It can feel impossible to form another connection with another person ever again while you are in a codependent relationship, therefore being unwilling to leave your partner.

You must remember that you matter. Your feelings and your well-being are very important. When you aren't being treated fairly, even being abused, you need to realize that you deserve more than this. When your partner shows you that he or she cares about you, this shouldn't be through abuse or manipulation. It should be through the love that you crave. The cycle will only continue to repeat the longer that you stay a part of it. If you are struggling in a relationship like this, tell someone that you trust. Getting help does not have to happen all at once, it can start with small steps. Telling someone else about what you are going through is like letting go of a little bit of the burden. You shouldn't have to carry the weight of it all on your own. If you ever feel that you are in immediate danger, you need to make sure that you contact the proper authorities and get yourself to a safe space before something worse happens to you. The seriousness of an abusive relationship should not be underestimated.

Chapter 9: Empath and Narcissistic Relationships

As mentioned previously, the difference between an empath/narcissist relationship and a codependent relationship is that the abuse is normally one-sided. In the former, one person takes on a clear role as the dominant partner while the other person remains submissive. There is no manipulation or control happening on behalf of the submissive person because that is just not in an empath's nature. Instead, an empath would sooner stay in the toxic situation before speaking up against his or her partner. Because they feel things so strongly and compassionately, it is difficult to just walk away from the things that are bothering them. Though they know that they aren't being treated fairly, something inside of them doesn't let go of the fact that they love and care about their partner. This creates a dynamic that becomes incredibly toxic for both parties involved.

The narcissistic individual might care about their partner, as narcissists are able to successfully maintain romantic relationships. However, they come first in their own life. They are never going to be the considerate and caring partner that the empath craves. Instead, they are going to live their life as they see fit. When they want something, they will stop at nothing to put themselves first so that they will get it. Even if their partner expresses their unhappiness at the unfair treatment, because the narcissist feels no empathy, their behavior is unlikely to change. This is the ultimate definition of a controlling relationship. The other person naturally relinquishes control of his or her freedom in order for their partner to receive all of the personal gains.

Because an empath comes from such a caring place, he or she will be quick to defend their partner if anyone on the outside ever questions the relationship. You can count on them to have an explanation or some kind of reasoning, even if it doesn't make much sense. An empath does not like to admit when things are too much to handle. Instead, they will sooner internalize all of the negativity than admit that they need help processing it. This suppression of emotions puts them at risk of an emotional outbreak waiting to happen. Because their narcissistic partner has no consideration for their feelings, their partner can very quickly send them into a dark downward spiral. Still, the empath will likely just continue to put up with the abuse because they will convince herself that they deserve to be treated this way.

Though the dynamic between an empath/narcissist relationship differs from a codependent one, there are some definite crossovers that can be seen in both. When you are able to understand the dynamics of one, it becomes easier to understand the other. What is most important with controlling relationships is that they need to be acknowledged. The more that everyone ignores the abuse, the more it will continue to occur. Whether you are in the relationship yourself or witnessing it on the outside, getting the courage to speak up can be very difficult. If you want what is best for you and for the person that you care about, know that it is necessary to break the cycle. Something needs to change in order for the abuse to stop.

How Labels Are Hindering

WHILE WE ARE ALL FAMILIAR with the textbook definitions of the terms narcissist, codependent, and empath, there is a certain structure of thinking that is important to let go of. Most of us would be quick to judge that the narcissist is for sure the most evil of the three, always responsible for wrongdoing. There is a natural stigma built up around the concept of narcissism because it is the most outwardly destructive personality type. Ironically, the seriousness of being a narcissist has also made its way into our cultural norms. People are quick to self-label themselves as narcissists because they enjoy looking in the mirror. It is important to understand that narcissism goes beyond vanity. When we casually throw the label around, it promotes a whole new kind of stigma that suggests a narcissist can simply stop what they are doing.

Narcissism defines a set of behaviors, and as mentioned, these behaviors extend beyond vanity. They are often cocky and persuasive individuals with a deep underlying sense of insecurity. Desperate for validation, they will resort to manipulative or even abusive tendencies in order to get what they want. This is an incredibly selfish person who will patronize anyone in order to feel superior. Outward appearance is everything to a narcissist. This person is never going to let anyone on the outside know that he or she is struggling with insecurity. Instead, they are going to put on a front that alludes to their amazing success and effortless accomplishments.

An empath is someone with a gift. This is a person who is able to put themselves in someone else's situation in order to act accordingly. Empathy itself is a trait that many people have, some more than others. A defining characteristic of a narcissist is that the person lacks empathy entirely; therefore, they are able to use people around him or her in order to get what they want. To be an empath, you must be especially tuned in to the way that other people think. It can be a blessing and a curse to feel everything so strongly, and it can sometimes lead to being taken advantage of because of the willingness to relate to others. You can see how a narcissist and an empath would fit together based on the two distinct personalities that were described.

There isn't necessarily a clear way to spot a narcissist or an empath. On the outside, the traits aren't particularly clear. It is when you are in a relationship with someone that you get to know a deeper level to who they are. To each person, their behavior is entirely justified. Whether a person acts as an aggressor or a victim, each set of actions is something that makes sense to them. They each play a role in the bigger picture of the relationship, acting according to their prominent traits. A lot of people believe that empaths are always better people. They are known for being caring, and they just want to understand others, so of course one would assume that they are always the victims of horrible situations.

Where Codependency Fits In

YOU MIGHT BE WONDERING how codependency ties into narcissism and empathy. Take a moment to think about which personality type that a codependent individual would be most likely to have. Are they in it for themselves or do they act the way that they do for the sake of someone that they care about? You should be able to see that the answer is the latter. Remembering the traits of codependency, this is an individual who acts in the "best interest" of their partner. Whether they truly are looking out for their partner, or just doing these things because they are acting on their empathy, they are not looking for an end result that necessarily benefits them. This is how being an empath can result into something negative. None of these categories are concrete, though. There is absolutely a way for a codependent individual to act like a narcissist when necessary.

Codependent individuals have the capacity to control their partners when they feel like they need to be in charge of a situation. As mentioned, abuse can happen at the hands of the destructive individual as well as the codependent individual. When a person acts this way, they are actually acting on their narcissistic tendencies. In this way, a codependent individual can also be a narcissistic individual. This is why labels are not necessarily an accurate way to categorize people. We are all so complex, and we have the ability to change based on our surroundings. In this way, you can see that all of the traits are interconnected and situational. Depending on the environment that we put ourselves in, we tend to choose our own coping mechanisms.

No matter which role a person takes on, accountability is important. This is one thing that people are normally all incapable of when they find themselves in a codependent relationship. Because neither one sees anything wrong with their behavior, they become unwilling to make any changes. They are also relying on the dynamic in order to feel comfortable and to survive, so they would see no reason to make any changes despite underlying dissatisfaction that is felt. Both parties are going to feel like they are the victim in the situation. They are both going to have their own proof as to why they are victims, believing that the other person is entirely in the wrong. This is an exhausting and never-ending cycle of toxicity.

If you feel as though you may be empathetic and dealing with empath/narcissist relationships, you can find a wealth of information on the topic in the companion book to this one titled, "Toxic Magnetism," by myself, Kara Lawrence. This book is the only one of its kind in that it is the only book that attempts to explain the root cause of this very common attraction dynamic that so many codependents experience.

Label Culture

IN TODAY'S SOCIETY, it has almost become trendy to throw around the terms narcissist, empath, and codependent without fully understanding their dynamics and relationships. People like to assign empaths as victims and narcissists as abusers. While there is a lot more to the dynamic, it has become a social norm to talk about these individuals in this way. Codependency has also become a term that is thrown around casually, often describing a relationship where two people spend a lot of time with one another. While this is an aspect of true codependency, you know that this is not the only defining factor. Codependency is a much deeper issue that can often lead to abuse. People who have never truly experienced it are able to find it easy to throw the label around, even when it doesn't necessarily apply.

With the ease of access to the basic definitions of these terms, people mistake this knowledge as a true representation of each role. You will come to find that it is nearly impossible to fully understand them all unless you have personally been involved in a similar situation. In order to stop this misrepresentation, self-diagnosing habits need to stop. When we are filled with knowledge about something new, we often believe that we know enough to know that we fit into a certain category. What usually happens is that a person is able to identify with a few of the *traits*, but not the true role. Therefore, it is not a true representation of being a narcissist, empath, or codependent.

To those who are truly suffering in a narcissist/empath relationship or a codependent relationship, their struggles might feel invalid because of the casual way and frequency that each term is used. Someone who doesn't see their condition as something serious is going to be even less likely to get help for the situation that they are in. Another thing that can happen is denial. Any of these personalities can rely on their own denial as a reason for not making a change in their situation. To them, nothing is truly wrong, so there would be no need to change anything about the relationship. This is a very skewed viewpoint to have about issues that are so serious, and it is, unfortunately, being continually perpetuated by the way that society is so quick to throw all of the labels around.

In order to help with the stigma that surrounds all of these labels, it is important to only use the term to describe yourself when you have been diagnosed by a professional. It is okay to say that you have narcissistic *tendencies* but claiming that you are a narcissist is likely not accurate due to the actual defining characteristics of narcissism. It is also important that you aren't quick to place labels on other people or their relationships. Even when you know that a situation is unhealthy, your priority should be to extend a hand in order to help. The labels are less important when a situation is so serious. The best thing that you can do is to speak up when you feel like something is not right, whether it be in your own relationship or someone in a relationship that you care about.

Chapter 10: Solutions to Codependency Issues: Must I End My Relationships?

The paths that you can take when you realize that you are in a codependent relationship are simple—either fix the relationship or end it. While these things are easier said than done, they are the only viable solutions. The latter is the preferable option because it is important for a codependent individual to learn how to be happy alone. When you are without the influence of a person that you used to rely on, you will be able to learn how to survive. It is almost as though you need to start over from the very beginning, relearning the foundations of how to live. Without the need to make your own decisions in a codependent relationship, you would be surprised at how easy it can be to forget how to do this all together. Because you have been so used to another person dictating your life (you have actually enjoyed this), your basic perception of right and wrong has usually been removed. When you see choices presented in front of you, there is no inner-voice that kicks in to tell you what needs to be done.

This is why codependency can become so dangerous. You are giving so much of yourself to another person that you forget how to function on your own. Naturally, this is not the desired feeling and you will probably go to any length that you can in order to save the relationship before you walk away. This is what got you into this situation in the first place. Your desire to stay will greatly outweigh your desire to end the relationship. When you know deep down that you are ready to make a big change and regain control over your life, you need to consider the following four methods to help get you back on your feet:

- **Abstinence**: In the same way that an alcoholic must give up alcohol, you need to be willing to give up the person that is creating all of the negativity in your life. This is a step that is very necessary to successfully recover from codependency. Your main goal is to turn your attention inward, toward yourself. Because you have been so focused on your partner, this might feel like a betrayal. What you need to remember is that your own happiness can only be maintained if you do something to help yourself. No matter how much you help other people, your partner included, your needs are never going to be met. While cutting off communication entirely isn't normally a realistic option in most codependent relationships, a severance is still necessary. You need to establish the fact that you are your own person and that you no longer want to be in a relationship with your partner. This is likely going to cause some backlash, maybe even a dramatic display of emotions on behalf of your partner. You need to remain strong, though. Remember how trapped you feel in your current situation and envision yourself living a happy life that is exactly what you want it to be. Your partner is also going to benefit from this severance, realizing that he or she cannot use other people in order to control their happiness. They also need to find their own.

- **Awareness**: Denial is the number one thing that is going to hold you back on your journey toward a healthy relationship. Denying that there is a problem is likely how you have gotten to this toxic point in your current relationship. Both of you have probably become accustomed to thinking that there is nothing wrong with the way you operate. It works for you, so it must be fine. Take accountability for your own actions. While you cannot force your partner to do the same, you need to realize which of your own behaviors are enabling. If you are a codependent person, there is definitely at least one thing that you are doing that is enabling your partner's destructive behavior. It might seem like you are simply being caring and supportive, but deep down, you probably know what it is that you are doing. Enabling behavior is something that gives your partner a go-ahead, telling him or her that they are acting in a way that they should. It is something that will give them encouragement or validation to act in a way that only serves them and their needs. Think about all of the things that you have done throughout the relationship that has only served your partner. You need to be aware that this is part of the problem, the reason why you are in this current situation.

- **Acceptance**: In order to heal, you don't need to harshly punish yourself until you feel enough guilt for what you have allowed. Instead, you need to do the opposite. Acceptance is essential for getting better. Because you cannot go back in time to change the things that you have done or allowed, you need to accept them for what they are. Acknowledge the things that you have done and see them for what they are without judging yourself. It takes a lot of courage to take a look at yourself so honestly, and a lot of strength to be able to do so without judgment attached. The more that you resist a situation, the harder it is going to fight back. This means, if you simply try to resist your codependent relationship, you are going to only be pulled further in. You need to fully accept everything that you have been going through in order to realize that you want to make a change. This change is something that is going to be very real, and not a mere temporary fix. Getting to the root of the dysfunctional behavior and eliminat-

AM I CODEPENDENT? AND WHAT DO I DO ABOUT IT?

ing it is what you need to do if you are going to see any progress.

- **Action**: When you have enough insight to inspire you to make a change, the action comes next. This is the process of actually doing something that will result in a change. Moving into your own place is an example of taking action. It is a decision that you make that will put distance between you and the person who has taken control over your life. When you are responsible for your own living situation, you are going to have to make decisions. This is a great way to re-enter a rational way of thinking. Because you are going to be so focused on getting back on your feet and doing whatever it takes, your mind isn't going to be dwelling on your past relationship. While it is normal to feel grief over everything that you have been through and probably even miss the person that you were with, there is nothing better than giving yourself something to do if you would truly like to get over the relationship. This is your chance to correct all of the wrongdoing that you have been programmed to think is the only way to live. By navigating through your new life, you will be forced to re-learn all of the skills necessary in order to get by. This can be an incredibly challenging and lonely time, especially when you were so used to relying on someone else to do these things for you. Make sure that you have a strong support system who will keep encouraging you along the way.

Though codependency is thought of as a relationship problem in modern times, you must realize that codependency actually stems from your own behavior. Even if you have major issues with your partner, you need to be able to take accountability for your own actions that contribute to these issues. It isn't a standard relationship problem that can be discussed once and then forgotten about. Because codependency is a lifestyle and, to some, a disease, there is more work to be done. You must understand that the signals you send your partner are a contributing factor to your codependent relationship. While you shouldn't harbor all of the blame, you need to understand that you play a big role in dysfunction too. This is why it is important for you to truly take action when it comes to ending and healing from a codependent relationship.

This kind of breakup is going to be different than a traditional one. With other breakups, there is usually a point where you realize that you do not want to be together anymore. You are then able to remember why you are not compatible right now, grieve the relationship, and then move on. With codependency, you need to make the conscious choice to pry yourself away. You might not feel ready to end the relationship; it might feel like the worst decision in the world to you. It might even result in making you feel as though you can't continue living without your partner. This is why you should end things before they progress to the point of total debilitation. Codependency takes away parts of you each day, and soon, you won't be left with anything at all. When your partner has all of the control or causes you to crave the control, you are both acting from a place of power. Gaining control is what will cause a person to feel satisfied in a codependent relationship, not love and care. When your needs aren't being met, it makes sense that you would need to strive for something else that is meant to keep you "happy." It is all just a power struggle.

Breaking up is not always going to be the solution. Each relationship is different, despite its codependent label. When people are involved in a relationship like this, chances are that it has already become toxic by the time one person decides that a change is needed. Reeling back this type of behavior is extremely difficult and can cause a lot of tension between the individuals. The best way to heal is to learn how to be on your own. To a codependent person, there is a huge stigma around doing anything alone. It is what is necessary to re-learn the essentials of daily living, though. The satisfaction that you will get when *you* meet your own needs is unbeatable. Before anyone else is able to give you that, you should be able to give it to yourself because you deserve it.

Relationship Reform

IF YOU FEEL THAT BREAKING up with your partner is not a realistic option, for safety concerns or genuine inability, then the first thing that you must do is set boundaries. This is an immediate change that needs to happen when you decide that you are going to try to work things out. Because a codependent relationship is so unequal, you will want to distribute more power to the person who does not have any. Set boundaries that you feel are reasonable and that make you happy. You need to be thinking about your own needs, the deepest desires that you are too afraid to share with your partner. When you have any conversations about your relationship, make sure that both of you are taking them seriously. Talk about things in a quiet, private setting. Don't end the conversation before coming up with some kind of a solution that you can try together.

Working on a relationship takes commitment. It is great if you feel like you are strong enough to change things and work on them for the better, but you must make sure that your partner does too. If you aren't on the same page, your efforts will be in vain. There is no need to push yourself to any limits if you know that your partner doesn't feel the same way. There should be no convincing him or her to change or asking them to re-think the relationship. If they feel the way that you do, then they will already be on board when you mention that you would like to work on things. Therapy is a great option for couples. It provides you with a safe space to sort through your issues while in the presence of an outside source to act as a mediator. A lot of couples claim that therapy is what saved their relationship. A therapist is going to be able to help see things from another perspective, informing you both of the patterns that are seen within your relationship. It can be a very insightful and helpful experience.

Communication is absolutely necessary when working through codependency issues. If you feel something, you must not suppress it. Tell your partner exactly how his or her behavior is making you feel and vice versa. The entire problem of codependency stems from the fact that you are acting as an enabler. Remember, when you don't say anything about behaviors that bothers you, you are enforcing it. By speaking up to your partner, you are going to show him or her that you are not okay with being treated like an option in their life. You deserve to be made a priority. When they act out in ways that you do not

AM I CODEPENDENT? AND WHAT DO I DO ABOUT IT?

understand, confront them about it. Try to get some insight as to why they feel the need to do these things. You don't have to get into an argument about it but do your best to dig deeper and find out what they are actually thinking. In a way, the two of you must rebuild your trust. Anything that is left standing is only there because of an unequal dynamic. There should be a fair chance to express oneself from both sides of the relationship, and a priority must be placed on the way that you treat one another.

Chapter 11: Exercises

No matter what your journey looks like, you are going to need time to heal from codependency. Whether you end the relationship or decide to work it out with your partner, what matters most when it comes to healing is that you feel whole and well-rounded. You need to be healthy in a physical, spiritual, and emotional sense. These exercises are meant to take your old habits and turn them into productive new ones that are meant to serve you well. By the time you have completed your healing journey, you should feel refreshed and renewed. If you did want to pursue a new relationship, you would be at a point to do so. It is very important that you take the time to go through the healing process, otherwise, it can be so easy to get back into a codependent relationship without even realizing it.

Positive Affirmations

AS YOU NAVIGATE THROUGH your healing, it is a good idea to create some sort of mantra for yourself. This can be recited when you are having difficulties moving on, or when you simply need a reminder of how you deserve to be treated. Positive affirmations are entirely personal, so you can come up with any mantra to recite something that will make you feel good. To start, if you are unable to think of one, you can use this: "I am a spiritual being full of light and love." This is going to remind you that you are trying your best and that you need to remain calm and positive about your situation. A mantra is great for giving yourself an extra boost of confidence when you need it most.

If you want to, you can create different mantras for different situations. Try out a few to discover what you respond best to. Healing from a codependent relationship involves a lot of work that must be done on yourself. It can feel overwhelming and confusing at times, so these positive affirmations are meant to make you feel like you have support. There is a lot of power in knowing that you can successfully support yourself and get through something that is so full of emotional turmoil. Your mantra will cause you to see yourself positively, which is exactly what you need as you try to learn and grow from the situation that you were in.

Inner Child Work

IMAGINE THAT YOU ARE yourself at 5-years-old, new to the world and still learning about its ways. Write down all the things that you believe that little girl deserves, never stopping until you feel that the list is complete. It is likely that you are going to be able to write down a lot of things. Now, write down some reasons why you deserve these things. Are you worthy of love? Do you have a great heart? Now, take a look at what you have written down, and recite everything aloud. Instead of mentioning the child, substitute those words to reflect your current self. You can try reading this in front of a mirror in order to make a bigger impact. As much as you believed in each kind word as you wrote it down for that 5-year-old version of yourself, think about how you are still the same person who is also deserving of all these good things.

This can be an emotionally challenging exercise. It might even make you feel uncomfortable, but it is what you need to do in order to truly believe that you deserve better treatment. You wouldn't let anyone abuse or take advantage of the child you once were, so why would you let this happen to yourself as an adult? Try to get to the root of this cause, exploring the various stages of your life. Is there any point that you actually betrayed yourself? Did you give up on striving for better treatment because of your controlling partner? This exercise will allow you to get to these answers if you are patient. You might need to practice this several times before you truly allow yourself to open up. Being vulnerable can be difficult, especially for those who were once in a codependent relationship.

Detachment

BODY LANGUAGE IS IMPORTANT in any interaction. It can say a lot about how a person is feeling. Pay attention to your own body language. This includes the way that you stand, the amount of eye contact that you make, and the gestures that you incorporate into your conversations. As you talk to different people, you can also study their body language. You will be able to tell a lot about someone by doing this simple observation. The more that you become familiar with various non-verbal cues, the better you will be able to understand yourself. You might find that you tell the same stories over and over again, or that you avoid eye contact because you are afraid to let people know exactly how you are feeling. As you become more aware of the things that you do, you will be able to be more honest with yourself.

As you become more aware of the way that you speak, you are actually detaching yourself from the person that you are speaking to and allowing yourself to have your own thoughts. Try to give the other person your own genuine reactions, free of influence. You might find that, within your codependent relationship, you were made to feel like you *had* to respond in a certain way or else it would cause a fight. Let go of the idea that you might accidentally say the wrong thing because your own thoughts and ideas are valid. Becoming aware of how you communicate is going to act as a reset button that will allow you to feel comfortable again.

Boundaries for Shame

AS A CODEPENDENT INDIVIDUAL, you are probably used to living in a constant state of shame. There is an internal struggle that happens when your partner seems as though he or she is never pleased with you, but you are also settling yourself short by not ensuring that your own basic needs are met. This can create a lot of toxic shame because you likely always feel like you are doing something wrong or making a mistake. This narrative is not your fault; being with a partner who tricks you into feeling this way can be extremely confusing once you are out of the relationship. As you work on your healing process, it is important that you untrain these behaviors. You need to draw a boundary between your codependent self and your true self. At first, this might sound impossible to you because you are only one person. Dig deeper and listen to what your shame is really telling you. What are the things that you wish you could've done or said?

While you should never entirely suppress your feelings, it is okay to let go of the shame. Accept that you once felt this way, and then make a commitment to yourself for something better. Know that you have the right to exist without being validated by your partner or another person. Any negative actions that were done to you were rooted in deep insecurity felt by the other person. There is nothing that you could've said differently or done differently because it was not right of that person to treat you that way in the first place. Just as you have healing to do, so do they. It is not your job to fix them, but you must make sure that you feel okay with yourself. Learn how to accept who you truly are as a person. Act as though you are starting from the beginning again, first getting to know yourself.

Positive Surroundings

THE PEOPLE THAT YOU choose to spend your time with as you are healing are going to make a big impact on you. Make sure that you keep your circle of people close during this time because allowing too much outside influence can become distracting. You will want to only associate with those you know have your best interest at heart. Spend time with the people that truly care about you and want to see you succeed. If you receive any negativity or blame from someone in your support system, you must reconsider why you are keeping them in your life at this time. Anything like this has the ability to further confuse you and delay your healing process. Those who truly care about you are going to be happy to see you take back your freedom. There should be no indication of jealousy or negativity involved.

Spend time with those who think the way that you would like to think. People with positive traits are great to be around. You will end up learning a lot when you spend time with others who are also involved in self-love. Having a mentor during this time is a great idea. This is a person who you should be able to rely on and turn to for advice. Your mentor should be someone that knows about your situation and can see a plan for your future. Working on treating yourself better with the help of someone else also holds you accountable for your actions.

Self-Expression

WRITING CAN BE A GREAT way to express yourself. It doesn't have to be formal or structured; freewriting is a very beneficial habit to get into. When you are freewriting, allow yourself to jot down each word exactly as it comes to your mind. Make sure that you choose a quiet location and set aside a certain amount of time for yourself. You can start out with 10 minutes in the beginning, but you will likely find that you will want to keep writing for longer than this. If you get into a regular habit of freewriting, your thoughts will become clearer and your emotions will become easier to express. Often, codependent individuals feel as though their freedom has been stripped away. Writing is one way to get it back and regain control. When you write, there are no rules that you must follow or expectations that you must meet. The exercise is solely about your own self-expression.

If you feel like writing doesn't do the trick, you can search for different ways to express yourself. Dance and art are two other valid options that you can choose. Anything that promotes creativity is going to be a healthy way to get used to living your own life again. Self-expression is important because you get to show people exactly who you are. You also get to learn a lot about yourself. There should always be at least one activity that you can rely on in your life to give you an ultimate sense of freedom. Creative activities tend to fit these needs very well. Try out different hobbies until you find the one that is perfect for you. It might take some trial and error before you are able to find your ideal match.

Loving Yourself

BEING ABLE TO SAY THAT you love yourself is a positive step that requires a lot of effort. When you are in a codependent relationship for so long, you might actually forget how to love yourself. Codependency forces you to push your own needs into the background while you focus on your partner's. Anything that you want isn't going to be a priority. So, how do you turn the focus back onto yourself after you are out of a

AM I CODEPENDENT? AND WHAT DO I DO ABOUT IT?

codependent relationship? You might be lost with how to begin your journey of self-love. All of the stress that has built up over the duration of your relationship is now going to be felt as you are trying to navigate through life independently. It might be difficult to even determine a single thing that you love about yourself. The process doesn't happen overnight, so don't add unnecessary pressure to your situation.

If you are at a loss for words, take some time to sit down by yourself and make a list of all the things that you are good at. What are some traits that you find admirable in yourself? Are you great with people? Do you enjoy utilization skills? By letting your guard down, you will be able to acknowledge the things that you excel in. Be kind to yourself and try your best not to pass unnecessary judgment. Negativity isn't going to help you succeed as an independent person. You need to be your own support system until you can seek out others who support you, as well. The lesson to learn is that you should be able to rely on yourself before you rely on anyone else.

Chapter 12: Happy Being Me

Achieving happiness revolves around your ability to be happy as the person that you are. Being able to say that you feel true happiness should mean that you don't need to rely on anyone in order to reach this point. Being self-sufficient is the state of being that you should try to achieve. You should be able to meet all of your needs, first and foremost, before anyone else does. Whenever you do meet the right person who will do these nice things for you, they will be much more appreciated. Remember that your happiness comes from within. It is always going to come from within, no matter what you are currently going through. This can be hard to believe when you have been so used to living for another person. Trust in yourself and know that you have the ability to make yourself happy. By using these methods, you can learn how to truly love yourself:

- **Have Fun Alone**: There are so many things that we do for fun in which we mistakenly let ourselves believe that we need another person to do them with. Show yourself that you are able to have fun without the help of anyone else. Take yourself out to a movie or go see a concert. Things that you enjoy doing should be fun regardless of who you are with if you are with anyone at all. Being comfortable with being alone becomes easier when the situation is lighthearted. Having fun is a welcome distraction when you are dealing with the grief from your codependent relationship.

- **See the World**: Allow yourself the chance to take a solo trip. You don't need to fly across the country in order to have this experience. Even a simple road trip into the next town can be enough to feel the travel bug. When you are able to see other perspectives, you will be able to scale your problems down to an appropriate level. The point of taking trips alone is to get to spend some quality time with yourself. You will get to do exactly what you want to do when you want to do it. A lot of people find that they really enjoy traveling alone from time to time because it allows them the chance to learn more about themselves.

- **Get Rid of Your Comfort Zone**: When you are able to break free of your usual routine, this is when the best self-discovery tends to happen. Try your best to say yes to things that you normally would not say yes to. Give yourself a chance to experience all of the things that you have been too scared to do while you were involved in your codependent relationship. There are probably some things that come to mind that you believe you have missed out on. Learning how to love yourself is your chance to take back these moments that you deserve and experience the things that you have always wanted.

- **Make Time for Relaxation**: Downtime is important to have; we all need it if we want to function at our full capacity. Make use of this time by treating yourself to some relaxation. A lot of the time, our free time gets filled with errands or more tasks to complete. Try to make room for at least a few hours of relaxation a week. Whether this is treating yourself to a massage at the spa or a relaxing soak in a hot tub, you deserve to unwind and reset your mind. While life can be unpredictable, you need to make sure that you always make at least a little bit of time for relaxation.

- **Learn How to Say No**: Saying no is a big step when it comes to learning how to love who you are. We all have the ability to feel pressured by other people into acting a certain way. When we might be exhausted beyond belief, all it takes is a convincing request before we are over-exerting ourselves when we really didn't have to. It is your right to say no when you want to. You do not have to feel guilty for doing so. Practicing this gives you back your power. It allows you the chance to make your own decisions.

- **Acknowledge Your Accomplishments**: When you do something right, praise yourself for it! You deserve to feel proud of all you accomplish. Instead of waiting on other people to validate you, give yourself the recognition that you deserve. By hearing all of the positive things that you are capable of, you will inevitably learn how to love yourself more. We could all use reminders every so often about what we are able to achieve. Take matters into your own hands by expressing your support for yourself.

- **Create a Vision Board**: Your vision board should be a visual collection of your goals. You can cut photos out of magazines or even draw them if you are feeling up to it. Gather as many examples that you can of your ideal life and place them together on a board that you can reflect on often. Once you complete your vision board, you can place it in a spot where you will be sure to see it every day. It will serve as a reminder of what is possible when you learn how to love yourself.

- **Practice Self-Care Often**: Self-care is essential if you want to feel positively toward yourself. If you claim that you are on a journey of self-love, yet you do not respect your physical and mental state, then it is going to be hard to acquire trust for yourself. Your actions have to match the words that you say. Listen to what your body and mind truly need. Make sure that you are meeting these needs on a regular basis, and check-in with yourself often.

Self-Soothing

THE WAY THAT WE LEARN to calm ourselves down when we are babies is what can be described as self-soothing. It can be difficult for a baby to feel comfortable enough to sleep through the night on his or her own. There are different ways that parents aim to teach their child how to self-soothe, and this can greatly impact how he or she handles their emotions as an adult. The idea behind self-soothing is that the child is meant to learn how to do this on their own. They must learn how to do things that make them feel better. A parent can only give a child the love and support, but ultimately, self-soothing is to be learned independently. A child who has mastered the art of self-soothing is going to be one who is able to stay asleep when they are placed in their crib. If they wake up in the middle of the night, they will find comfort in their surroundings in order to fall back asleep.

A parent helps the child learn how to do this by creating a bedtime routine. This routine establishes a sense of security around bedtime. This is a time that is supposed to be safe and relaxing with no stressors involved. When we form these habits at a young age, we are going to be more likely to continue them into adulthood. The routine should be made up of a few different steps, but it doesn't have to be overly complicated. It can include something like getting into pajamas and then reading a bedtime story. When a baby knows what to expect as nighttime falls, he or she is going to be less likely to be fussy.

We can take the self-soothing techniques that we learned as children and use them well into adulthood. If you are feeling overwhelmed by life, utilize the methods that you were taught. Put on your favorite comfortable attire and get yourself in a relaxed state of mind. Whether you enjoy reading or sitting back and watching one of your favorite shows, your goal is to get into a mindset where you can let yourself rest without holding onto any negativity or anxiety. If you were never taught these things during childhood, it isn't too late to learn them now. Find the things that allow you to let your guard down and experience some vulnerability.

Enjoy Alone Time

BEING ALONE IS OFTEN stigmatized as something that should feel lonely or uncomfortable. In reality, spending time alone is extremely healthy for maintaining your self-love. When you do things alone, you are in total control of the situation. You get to decide what you would like to do and when you would like to do it. By eliminating the outside factors that are usually involved, you must place your trust in yourself in order to have a great time alone. This can be a scary concept, especially for someone who is coming directly out of codependency. Start small at first so that you do not overwhelm yourself. You do not need to seclude yourself for hours at a time, forcing solitary time. Do what feels right to you.

Being able to sit at home and simply enjoy your own company is a great starting point. Get rid of all distractions that allow you to communicate with other people. You might have to put your phone in the other room in order to avoid being tempted to text or call a friend. Watch TV, write in your journal, or cook yourself a meal. Doing any of these things can qualify as having some alone time. As you become more comfortable, you can try to leave your house and do things like go out to eat or explore a museum. The more you spend time by yourself, the more comfortable t you will be with yourself. This makes it easier to practice self-love.

You will really get a chance to learn about your likes and dislikes as you spend time by yourself. Being involved in codependency can often erase these parts about yourself. Don't feel alarmed if you feel like you have lost touch with yourself on this level. You still have the ability to learn about who you are. You might discover some things about yourself that you never knew before, causing you to fall in love with yourself. It is a great feeling when you are able to surprise yourself in such a positive way like this. Do not mistake self-love for selfishness. While you play certain roles in other people's lives, you also play a role in your own life. Don't be ashamed to get to know this individual. It can be hard to let your guard down, but it will happen over time. It is very important that you practice a lot of patience as you explore this next chapter in your healing process. Much like self-soothing, no one else is going to be able to spend this time alone with yourself. You are the one who must facilitate the action.

Separation from the Outcome

AS YOU AIM TO LIVE a happy life while doing the things that you want to do, it is important that you live in the moment. This is a cliché that you have probably heard countless times, but it is a helpful trick to overcoming your codependent habits. Codependency revolves around the "what ifs." You probably spent a lot of your time in your relationship thinking about what would happen if your partner left you, or what would happen if your partner got angry. This is a way of living that stems from worrying about the past or future. It was likely impossible for you to focus on the present because of your worries.

When you choose to become a happier person, you are choosing to live your life while remaining separated from the outcome. This means that you are consciously acknowledging that you cannot control every aspect of your life; there are too many outside factors involved. Awareness is still required, but you also must learn when to let go of your worries. If you know that you are a good person, and you love yourself, you can trust that you will make the best decisions that you can. By also surrounding yourself with great people, this is your way of gaining as much control over your environment as you can. These are the small things that you can guarantee but know that there is a lot in life that is not a guarantee.

If you are having trouble with your separation from the outcome, consider what might be holding you back. There is probably a lot of suppressed worry that you are still dealing with, especially if you have just recently ended your codependent relationship. Work through these feelings by allowing yourself to feel them, but only allow yourself to stay in this mindset for a certain amount of time. You deserve to take the time to process what you are feeling, but you must also make it a point to move on. If you never move on, your life is never going to move forward. Momentum is what will take you to the next step. Gravitate toward the things that make you feel good and acknowledge the things that don't without giving over your power to them.

Are you enjoying this book? Please consider leaving a review!

Chapter 13: Life After Codependency

After you have been living independently for a little while, be sure that you check in with yourself often. Make sure that you are still abiding by the new habits that you have put in place for yourself. Determine if you are feeling happier than

AM I CODEPENDENT? AND WHAT DO I DO ABOUT IT?

you used to feel before. Healing from a codependent relationship takes time, and you might have to try different methods in order to truly live for yourself. Remember, your life does not end just because your codependent relationship did. The more you are able to live your life and remain happy, the more growth you will see. Consider these things when you are checking in with yourself:

- **Are Your Needs Being Met?**: Consider the things that you do for yourself in order to ensure that you have what you want in life. Remember, obtaining what you want takes effort. A lot of the time, it can become easy to turn your focus onto another person, even after getting out of a codependent relationship. For example, you might try to make your friends' needs a priority over your own because you still have the habit of ignoring your needs. Make sure that you are not simply finding someone else to become codependent with. Know that you need to truly care about yourself and about the things that you need in order to make them happen. Pay attention to your emotions on a daily basis because they can be helpful in letting you know what you need more of.

- **Are You Having Fun?**: The healing process does not only have to feel like work. While you are going to be working on yourself, you also need to balance this out with some fun. Make sure that you are doing activities that allow you to have fun. Spend time with others who are lighthearted and seeking the same activities. There is nothing wrong with letting loose and being happy. While in a codependent relationship, you likely didn't have many experiences like this that solely revolves around your own fun. You have probably forgotten how good it feels to get in some laughter. The more that you are able to laugh and smile, the more you are actually balancing your body's chemistry. This is why having fun is beneficial not only for your mental health but also for your physical health.

- **Are You Still Protecting Yourself?**: Getting over a codependent relationship teaches you that it is alright to let your guard down. Through letting this wall down, you are going to be able to learn more about who you are as a person. It gives you the chance to truly strive toward what you want out of life. As you begin feeling comfortable with interacting with others again, you still need to make sure that you are protected. While you don't need to bring your walls back up, you do need to be aware of everybody's intentions with you. Consider if the person is spending time with you for personal gain, or if they truly enjoy your company. Take note on the balance within the interaction; are you getting a fair chance to express yourself and your opinions? When you are living for yourself, you must also take care of yourself and keep your best interests in mind.

AM I CODEPENDENT? AND WHAT DO I DO ABOUT IT?

If something is causing you negativity or heartache, do your best to avoid it.

- **Do You Accept Who You Are?**: As you begin your journey of healing and self-love, you are still probably going to be holding back a little. It is through time that you really get settled into becoming the person that you want to be. This is why checking in with yourself regularly is important. You need to ask yourself if you still accept the things that make you who you are. Changes are to be expected, but you must make sure that these changes align with your morals and values. Are you doing things because you want to? Or are you doing them because you feel like you have to? Answering these questions honestly can save you a lot of trouble in the future. You will learn what you need to do in order to make yourself feel more comfortable.

- **Are You Being Gentle?**: The healing process is naturally going to be intense with codependency. From the very beginning, it is a huge change to live for yourself and not for your partner. You are going to need to step up and begin making decisions right away or else your life is going to remain stagnant. Because all of this will continue to be a struggle during your healing, make sure that you are being as gentle on yourself as you can. There is no need to punish yourself or to put yourself down if you miss your partner or the codependent life that you used to have. This is perfectly *normal*. We would all miss it if it were our lifestyle for an extended period of time. Be kind to yourself, and make sure that your inner-voice matches your actions. It can become very easy to settle into a negative headspace when you are constantly putting yourself down.

- **Do You Consider Yourself Your Biggest Fan?**: It is okay to celebrate your accomplishments. In fact, it is encouraged! Allow yourself to feel pride in knowing that you are overcoming codependency each day. Every decision that you make for yourself is getting you one step closer to living independently. Some days are going to be harder than others, but what matters is that you are getting through them all. When you are trying your best, it is encouraged to acknowledge this. Creating a reward system can also be beneficial. When you reach certain milestones, allow yourself some indulgence. Eat your favorite foods, take a spa day, or go on a shopping spree. Do something that you have been looking forward to.

- **Are You Doing Well with Self-Expression?**: Being able to express what you like and dislike is essential. We are taught this skill as children, but it can become very easy to suppress once you become involved in codependency. Your goal is to re-learn self-expression. Figure out the things that you like and speak up about them. Let other people know why you like them and what causes you to feel this way.

AM I CODEPENDENT? AND WHAT DO I DO ABOUT IT?

If someone is doing something that you dislike, this is also a time to speak up. If you simply allow the behavior without correcting it, you are enabling it. That person isn't always going to know that you dislike it or that it is not okay with you. Don't be afraid to speak up because you have the right to do so.

- **Are You Being Passionate?**: You must give your life meaning. No one else is going to be able to assign things to you that you should feel passionate about. This is something for you to decide. Whether you are passionate about a sport or your job, gravitate toward things that will allow you to pursue your passions. This does not mean that you must revolve your life around these things, but they become great focal points for when you do not know what to do. Healing from codependency will likely take you to many places where you feel unsure about yourself and your actions but having your passions to fall back on can feel comforting.

Taking charge of your own life means living the way that you have always wanted to live. As long as you aren't hurting anyone in the process, there is no reason to feel guilty or ashamed. You deserve happiness just as much as everyone else in the world. By checking in with yourself regularly, you need to ask yourself the above questions. If you find that your answers don't line up, then there is always room for improvement. Make changes until you feel like you are truly living up to all of your expectations. If your needs are being met and you are participating in productive activities and habits, then you will automatically be destined for success. Your own greatness can attract additional greatness.

Remember, no one else is going to be able to make this change for you. It is truly a lifestyle change, and it is one that you need to work toward. Each day, you will be putting in effort towards your goals until they become a consistent part of your life. Just as easily as you settled into codependency, you can settle into a lifestyle that actually serves you. By living independently, you get to decide what happens. You get to decide the parameters for what is acceptable and unacceptable. It is important for people to reach this point because it serves as a reminder of how far life can take you. Being stuck in codependency limits what you feel you can do with your life. It allows you to believe that you cannot do more. Break free of this mindset by practicing your independent behaviors.

Getting Help

FOR SOME, RECOVERING from codependency is going to require additional help. This is nothing to feel ashamed of because codependency is a very serious condition. It alters the state of your brain and allows you to live a life that is based on ignoring your own needs and desires. This is a complex issue that can often feel too overwhelming to tackle on your own. While you can still practice all of the self-love exercises that have already been discussed, there is still an additional solution— talk to a professional. There are many options regarding what kind of treatment plan you can seek. Talk therapy is very beneficial to those who are feeling like they cannot successful-

AM I CODEPENDENT? AND WHAT DO I DO ABOUT IT?

ly live an independent lifestyle. A therapist is going to work through all of these worries and doubts with you. She or he will be able to guide you through them while offering practical solutions along the way. Therapy is like a big venting session that is made to encourage you to talk about the things that are hard to talk about.

A lot of codependent individuals seek out therapy because it is a simple solution to assist with the process of removing oneself from damaging relationships. Your therapist is going to provide you with a safe space where you will be able to say exactly what is on your mind. For many, therapy is one of the first places that the individual will remember the feeling of speaking up for themselves. Being silenced for so long can allow you to forget how to speak up. Your therapist is going to work with you by encouraging you to speak your mind and think deeply about your actions. It is an extremely beneficial treatment option that can be paired with the exercises that you already know how to do on your own. Your therapist can also hold you accountable for your progress. If you are actively trying to love yourself and do the things that make you happy, a therapy session is going to compliment this greatly.

If you do not feel comfortable with a one-on-one option, see if you can find any local support groups. A support group is set up like a therapy session with a professional present, but there are more people there who are struggling with the same issue. Through this type of treatment, you will be able to see that you are truly not alone in your struggles. The therapist is going to encourage you to talk if you want to talk. It might take you a few meetings before you are able to feel comfortable with speaking up, but that is okay. The point of a support group is to feel that you have a team behind you that has your back no matter what stage of the healing process you are in. It is through an environment like this one that you will be able to find strength through others. Hearing someone else's codependency story might be just what you need to inspire you to change your own.

Couples counseling is also a viable option if you are ending a codependent relationship but still staying with the same partner. As mentioned, this is a lot harder to overcome a lot of the time because the relationship is going to remain intact. Making changes while still being involved with the same individual might cause a lack of motivation or additional fighting. This is why seeing a therapist together can provide you with a chance to each speak about how you are feeling. The professional is going to act as a mediator that is willing to listen to both sides of the story. She is going to be able to offer you both advice and exercises to practice, but it ultimately comes down to the willingness from both of you in order to save the relationship. If you are both willing to make changes and seek help, then the relationship will stand a fighting chance. As much as you might want to fix things if your partner does not show any interest, then couples counseling isn't going to make a difference.

Conclusion

Through this guide, you have learned that codependent behavior can actually lead to a serious mental illness called dependent personality disorder (DPD). Those suffering from DPD experience the inability to take action in situations that require decision-making. The individual would much rather allow their partner to take control in order to not have any accountability over their own actions. There is also an inability to spend long periods of time alone. Codependent individuals thrive off of the support that they feel while being with their partners, so they are unlikely to act independently. DPD can become so severe that the codependent individual might feel that they never want to leave the house because they only wish to spend time with their partner. Friendships and other connections are often damaged due to this isolating behavior. When those on the outside express worry or concern over the situation, the codependent individual is likely to become defensive or angry. In their eyes, they must do everything they can in order to make their partner happy, even if it means sacrificing other aspects of their life.

While codependency is not actually a diagnosable condition, DPD is. Not everyone who exhibits symptoms of codependency is necessarily suffering from DPD, but they are surely on the path toward it. Only a medical professional can confirm such a diagnosis, but it is important to recognize the symptoms in yourself, your partner, or even someone else in your life that you care about. Often rooted in childhood abandonment issues, codependency leads an individual to believe that their needs come secondary to their partner's. The way that a relationship can become codependent is when this factor is mixed with their partner's destructive behaviors. Sometimes, but not always, the partner is actually a substance abuser. By acting codependently, the individual becomes an enabler to their partner's negative behavior.

There are two very clear roles in a codependent relationship—one person will make all of the decisions and the other will support their partner no matter what. This might seem like a one-sided arrangement, but it can be deceiving. The codependent individual can sometimes become just as controlling as their partner. Because they feel satisfaction from being needed, they will often try to manipulate situations in order to make their partner feel like they must always be kept around. Both individuals will begin to thrive on this dynamic. One person will display terrible behavior, and the other person will enable it. This is the type of relationship that becomes very set in their own ways, even when things start becoming toxic. There are instances where a codependent individual might refuse to leave the relationship, even despite abusive behavior at the hand of their partner. The dedication to the relationship is too strong to break free from.

It is clear to see that there is a big emphasis on the emotional health of the codependent individual. The partner will normally use this to his or her advantage, giving the individual attention that is being desired in order to continue on with the destructive behavior. This is just about the only need that is met in a codependent relationship, though. A codependent individual will become so invested in his or her partner that they even begins to ignore their basic need for happiness. Even when they desire more from their partner or wishes that he or she would stop their destructive ways, the codependent individual likely won't speak up in fear of losing the relationship. Instead, they suppress their own feelings further and further, until they eventually forgets about them. This becomes incredibly harmful, and it also puts the individual at risk of being in a long-term abusive situation. The codependent individual must be able to acknowledge that something needs to change within the relationship before he or she can get help. This is the hard part.

Signs to Pay Attention To

NOW THAT YOU ARE FAMILIAR with the concept of codependency, you are probably able to look at the warning signs and have a basic indication of the health of your own relationship. Remember, these are some behaviors that you will usually find within a codependent relationship:

- Making excuses for your partner's behavior
- Suppressed feelings of anger and resentment
- Frequent worry over your partner
- Inability to stand up against hurtful behavior
- Being influenced by your partner's mood
- Minimizing your own feelings

These are all examples of unhealthy behaviors that can stem from codependent relationships. The longer that these warning signs are ignored, the more intense the relationship is likely to become. Because things can spiral out of control so quickly, you might find that you are already in over your head once you realize that you can identify with the above traits. Some individuals are not only mentally incapable of ending a codependent relationship, but they also have a fear for their own well-being due to abuse. It can become a secret struggle that might never get the help it requires until the individual speaks up about what is going on. If you find that you are in a relationship similar to what is being described, tell someone you trust. This is the first step toward making any kind of change within your situation.

Being in a codependent relationship does not necessarily mean that you must be dating an addict, but the patterns are usually seen here. Remember, an individual can be addicted to a lot of different things. While alcohol and drugs are the main addictions that we tend to hear about, your partner can also be addicted to things like sex, gambling, shopping, and working. It is possible to become addicted to just about anything if the destructive behavior is present. In some cases, a codependent relationship can still form despite a lack of addiction. It is the kind of situation that can be very unpredictable. Never following the same exact guidelines, each case is going to be unique.

Codependency is not only found in romantic relationships. It can also be found in parent/child dynamics. Children who have grown up this way are more likely to gravitate toward a codependent relationship in the future because this is what they have always known. A codependent parental relationship can stem from being a part of a big family and feeling ignored, having one or more parents who is an addict, growing up feeling as though you aren't good enough, being told that you are not allowed to cry in order to express yourself, and feeling like no one cares about your well-being. These are all very difficult circumstances to grow up in, especially since a child is supposed to be full of wonder and curiosity. Codependency forces them to grow up with a sense of worry attached. Naturally, this behavior becomes very hard to correct if it has been occurring since childhood.

You can become involved in codependent relationships with your friends, too. When you have experienced hardship in the past, there is likely one friend that you have chosen to rely on. As you heal from your experience, that friend probably supported you every step of the way. From being there for you to vent to and providing you with uplifting speeches, it is nice to have someone like this in your life who cares so much. Much like all other codependent relationships, there is a fine line between this healthy behavior and codependency. While you are so reliant on your friend in order to get through a hard time, it might be difficult for you to separate yourself from this person. When he or she catches on, they might choose to display their destructive ways knowing that you need them just as much as they need you. This can become a tumultuous occurrence where you continually get hurt.

Because codependency is a learned behavior, it takes a lot of effort to unlearn. A person's past history can say a lot about their present habits. If someone has been going through codependency for years, it comes as no surprise when the behavior continues well into the future. This is a cycle that can be incredibly difficult to break, and the struggle can often occur in silence until the individual decides to express that they need help. The most important thing to remember is, despite a tough upbringing, a codependent individual chooses to serve his or her partner because they believe that it is "for their own good." This shows you that codependency is deeply rooted in a person's desire to be good enough for their partner. Any role that their partner needs to be filed, the individual is going to step up and fill it. They will continue doing this, even when they don't agree with the behavior. Therefore, a person's morals and values will be completely forgotten about.

A codependent individual achieves fulfillment through other people. Making dinner for themselves would not elicit the same feeling as making dinner for their partner. It is thought that, at some point in the individual's life, a source of pain was discovered. Whether this came from past trauma or a more recent hardship, this has caused a shutdown of the ability to care about themselves. Instead, all of the attention is put onto someone else. Caring for someone else allows the codependent individual to feel satisfied and useful. By entirely committing to their partner, the codependent individual will feel as though he or she has a true purpose in life again. Because our pain can often lead us to question our purpose, it makes sense that he or she would want to cling to this codependent behavior if it is the only thing that allows them to feel it.

Dangers Involved

WHILE CODEPENDENCY is a damaging trait to hold, you must remember that there are real dangers involved. This type of relationship can easily lead to abuse that is both verbal and physical. There are two ways that this normally tends to happen—the destructive individual will take advantage of their partner, or the codependent individual will aim to gain control over their partner. With the former, the abuse will likely happen the way you expect it to. Because the codependent individual is so submissive, this gives his or her partner a perfect opportunity to step in and fully take control. If their partner has narcissistic leanings, this means that they will only care to achieve personal gain, even if it means hurting the people around them. An individual like this will stop at nothing to get what they want, and because they have no desire to treat his or her partner right, the abuse is likely to happen.

There is a big connection between codependent relationships and narcissist/empath relationships. This dynamic is normally based on inequality from the beginning; therefore, it makes it easier for the dominant individual to take control. Even when the codependent individual tries to play off any abuse or makes excuses for their partner, the seriousness of the situation does not become any less severe. This is why it is important to speak up if you feel that you are experiencing something similar. If you see it happening to a person that you care about, do your best to let that person know that you are there to help. Approaching the situation too quickly can tend to scare people off or cause them to become more defensive. A simple caring approach is the best way to be supportive.

Abuse can also be seen in a different way. Sometimes, the codependent individual will become so controlling over his or her partner that they will choose to manipulate their partner in order to ensure that the relationship is going exactly the way that they want it to. Because they are codependent, they aren't going to be demanding of their own needs. Instead, the codependent individual will make it a point to allow their partner to believe that he or she cannot live without them and their help. It is their purpose to serve their partner, and they will become very protective over the relationship. If the codependent individual loses it, they will not know how to function on their own at first. This is a very big driving factor behind abuse that occurs from the other perspective.

Overall, codependency must be seen as a serious condition. Because it can become so destructive so quickly, getting help is important. While couples counseling is an option, the best way to get out of a codependent relationship is to end it. Through the help of self-love exercises and optional professional treatment, you will have the ability to get back on your feet and live your happiest life on your own terms. You must change your entire mindset into one that is positive and full of motivation. While this can seem hard at first, it is always possible. If you or someone that you know is struggling, encourage them with some steps in a positive direction. Break free of the cycle that holds you back and allow yourself to be treated well because that is what you deserve.

If you would like to further explore information on relationship dynamics and improving your dating and romantic life, consider the companion books in the series, written by myself, Kara Lawrence. "Toxic Magnetism," covers the hidden root cause of why sensitive people are so often attracted to narcissists and find themselves in repeating patters of unhealthy relationships. "Empath Awakening," can help sensitive people to stop absorbing the stress and negative emotion around them so they can live happier lives. And "Invisible Abuse" helps readers to understand the covert manipulation tactics of narcissists that can be difficult to spot without the proper knowledge.

If you enjoyed reading this book or have taken away something helpful in your life, please consider helping the author to produce more books like it by leaving a review. Thank you, and good luck on your journey to a healthy future!

References

Burney, R. (2015). Request Rejected. Retrieved from http://joy2meu.com/jump_start_recovery.htm

Lohmann, C.R. (2013). Codependency in Children. Retrieved from https://www.psychologytoday.com/us/blog/teen-angst/201310/codependency-in-children

Codependency Test | 9 Codependent Signs. (2014). [YouTube]. Retrieved from https://www.youtube.com/watch?v=OS1RP_-njwQ

Gunnars, K. (2018). 8 Common Symptoms of Food Addiction. Retrieved from https://www.healthline.com/nutrition/8-symptoms-of-food-addiction

Horton, M. (2018). 10 Warning Signs You're In a Codependent Relationship. Retrieved from https://psychcentral.com/blog/10-warning-signs-youre-in-a-codependent-relationship/

Hurst, K. (2019). How To Love Yourself And Be Confident With These 15 Self-Love Tips. Retrieved from http://www.thelawofattraction.com/love-yourself/

Jantz, G. (2018). Codependency and Emotional Abuse. Retrieved from https://www.psychologytoday.com/us/blog/hope-relationships/201810/codependency-and-emotional-abuse

Lancer, D. (2018a). 10 Ways to Love Yourself and Heal from Codependency - dummies. Retrieved from https://www.dummies.com/health/mental-health/codependency/10-ways-to-love-yourself-and-heal-from-codependency/

Lancer, D. (2018). Recovery from Codependency. Retrieved August from https://psychcentral.com/lib/recovery-from-codependency/

Ni, P. (2015). 14 Signs of Psychological and Emotional Manipulation. Retrieved from https://www.psychologytoday.com/us/blog/communication-success/201510/14-signs-psychological-and-emotional-manipulation

Rosenberg, R. (2018). The History of the Term, "Codependency." Retrieved from https://blogs.psychcentral.com/human-magnets/2013/11/the-history-of-the-term-codependency/

Smith, M. (2019). Narcissistic Personality Disorder - HelpGuide.org. Retrieved from https://www.helpguide.org/articles/mental-disorders/narcissistic-personality-disorder.htm

Sommer, C. (2019). Single Post | Grace Unfolding with Caitlin. Retrieved from https://www.graceunfoldingwithcaitlin.com/single-post/EMPATHS-VS-CODEPENDENTS-VS-NARCISSISTS

The Roots of Codependency - Outpatient Addiction Treatment. (2016). Retrieved from https://lastingrecovery.com/the-roots-of-codependency/

Vieira, K. (2019). Codependency vs. Dependent Personality Disorder. Retrieved from https://www.therecoveryvillage.com/mental-health/codependency/related/codependency-vs-dpd/

What Is Self-Soothing and Why Is it Beneficial? (2018). Retrieved from https://www.nycsleeptraining.com/what-is-self-soothing-and-why-is-it-beneficial/

www.ingramcontent.com/pod-product-compliance
Lightning Source LLC
Chambersburg PA
CBHW052059110526
44591CB00013B/2282